Overcoming Alcohol Problems

EDITOR-IN-CHIEF

David H. Barlow, PhD

SCIENTIFIC
ADVISORY BOARD

Anne Marie Albano, PhD

Gillian Butler, PhD

David M. Clark, PhD

Edna B. Foa, PhD

Paul J. Frick, PhD

Jack M. Gorman, MD

Kirk Heilbrun, PhD

Robert J. McMahon, PhD

Peter E. Nathan, PhD

Christine Maguth Nezu, PhD

Matthew K. Nock, PhD

Paul Salkovskis, PhD

Bonnie Spring, PhD

Gail Steketee, PhD

John R. Weisz, PhD

G. Terence Wilson, PhD

✓ Treatments *That Work*™

Overcoming Alcohol Problems

A COUPLES-FOCUSED PROGRAM

Therapist Guide

Barbara S. McCrady • Elizabeth E. Epstein

2009

OXFORD
UNIVERSITY PRESS

Oxford University Press, Inc., publishes works that further
Oxford University's objective of excellence
in research, scholarship, and education.

Oxford   New York
Auckland   Cape Town   Dar es Salaam   Hong Kong   Karachi
Kuala Lumpur   Madrid   Melbourne   Mexico City   Nairobi
New Delhi   Shanghai   Taipei   Toronto

With offices in
Argentina   Austria   Brazil   Chile   Czech Republic   France   Greece
Guatemala   Hungary   Italy   Japan   Poland   Portugal   Singapore
South Korea   Switzerland   Thailand   Turkey   Ukraine   Vietnam

Copyright © 2009 by Oxford University Press, Inc.

Published by Oxford University Press, Inc.
198 Madison Avenue, New York, New York 10016

www.oup.com

Oxford is a registered trademark of Oxford University Press

All rights reserved. No part of this publication may be reproduced,
stored in a retrieval system, or transmitted, in any form or by any means,
electronic, mechanical, photocopying, recording, or otherwise,
without the prior permission of Oxford University Press.

Library of Congress Cataloging-in-Publication Date

CIP data on file

ISBN 978-0-19-532287-3

9 8 7 6 5 4 3 2 1

Printed in the United States of America
on acid-free paper

About Treatments*ThatWork*™

Stunning developments in healthcare have taken place over the last several years, but many of our widely accepted interventions and strategies in mental health and behavioral medicine have been brought into question by research evidence as not only lacking benefit, but perhaps, inducing harm. Other strategies have been proven effective using the best current standards of evidence, resulting in broad-based recommendations to make these practices more available to the public. Several recent developments are behind this revolution. First, we have arrived at a much deeper understanding of pathology, both psychological and physical, which has led to the development of new, more precisely targeted interventions. Second, our research methodologies have improved substantially, such that we have reduced threats to internal and external validity, making the outcomes more directly applicable to clinical situations. Third, governments around the world and healthcare systems and policymakers have decided that the quality of care should improve, that it should be evidence based, and that it is in the public's interest to ensure that this happens (Barlow, 2004; Institute of Medicine, 2001).

Of course, the major stumbling block for clinicians everywhere is the accessibility of newly developed evidence-based psychological interventions. Workshops and books can go only so far in acquainting responsible and conscientious practitioners with the latest behavioral healthcare practices and their applicability to individual patients. This new series, Treatments*ThatWork*™, is devoted to communicating these exciting new interventions to clinicians on the frontlines of practice.

The manuals and workbooks in this series contain step-by-step detailed procedures for assessing and treating specific problems and diagnoses.

But this series also goes beyond the books and manuals by providing ancillary materials that will approximate the supervisory process in assisting practitioners in the implementation of these procedures in their practice.

In our emerging healthcare system, the growing consensus is that evidence-based practice offers the most responsible course of action for the mental health professional. All behavioral healthcare clinicians deeply desire to provide the best possible care for their patients. In this series, our aim is to close the dissemination and information gap and make that possible.

This therapist guide outlines a treatment program for couples wherein one partner has an alcohol use disorder (AUD). Based on the principles of CBT, this 12-session couples-focused program is designed not only to help the drinker stop drinking but also to help his or her partner change behaviors that may contribute to the drinker's problem. The third aim of treatment is to enhance the couple's relationship.

Over the course of the program, clients are taught to identify and modify high-risk situations and triggers for drinking, as well as how to change dysfunctional thoughts and feelings. The primary goal is complete abstinence from drinking. The partner is taught to identify and change behaviors that may contribute to the client's drinking, and the couple is taught skills for increasing positive interactions with one another and improving communication. In-session exercises and homework assignments help the couple stay motivated and provide an opportunity for teamwork. A relapse-prevention component helps the couple work together to develop a plan for handling slips or relapses and provides sound advice for managing the disorder well into the future.

Complete with step-by-step instructions for running sessions, as well as lists of materials needed, session outlines, and copies of forms necessary for treatment, this therapist guide provides you with all the information you need to successfully administer treatment for alcohol-use problems in a couples-therapy modality. Also available is a corresponding workbook for clients and their partners. Together, these books form a complete treatment package that clinicians will find to be a welcome addition to their armamentarium.

David H. Barlow, Editor-in-Chief,
Treatments *ThatWork*™
Boston, MA

References

Barlow, D.H. (2004). Psychological treatments. *American Psychologist, 59,* 869–878.

Institute of Medicine. (2001). *Crossing the quality chasm: A new health system for the 21st century.* Washington, DC: National Academy Press.

Dedication

To James F. Sachs (1913–2007) – my father, my teacher, my inspiration – BSM

To Jeremy, Eve, and Sam – who teach me the meaning and joy of devotion – EEE

To our patients – who constantly teach us courage, honesty, and hope

Acknowledgments

This therapist guide is the culmination of almost 30 years of work, and the contributions of countless colleagues, staff, and students. It is impossible to acknowledge them all by name, but we want especially to thank those who contributed to developing our treatment manuals and client worksheets, including: William Hay, David Abrams, Charles Neighbors, Barbara Niles, Sadi Irvine Delaney, Helen Raytek, and Melissa Mitchell. Staff and colleagues who have been key to the long-term success of our research program include: Nora Noel, Hilary Fisher-Nelson, Bob Stout, Sandy Hoffmann, Noelle Jensen, Sharon Cook, Jean Schellhorn, and Thomas Morgan. We are deeply grateful to them and to all who have contributed to our research program.

Contents

Chapter 1	Introductory Information for Therapists	*1*
Chapter 2	Clinical Issues in Alcohol Behavioral Couple Therapy (ABCT)	*25*
Chapter 3	Assessing Alcohol Use and Problems	*37*
Chapter 4	Session 1: Introduction / Rationale / Self-Recording	*55*
Chapter 5	Session 2: Functional Analysis / Noticing Positive Behavior	*91*
Chapter 6	Session 3: High-Risk Hierarchy / Partner Functional Analysis Part I / Self-Management Plans	*109*
Chapter 7	Session 4: Partner Functional Analysis Part II / Enhancing Motivation to Change	*125*
Chapter 8	Session 5: Dealing With Urges / Decreasing Partner Triggers	*135*
Chapter 9	Session 6: Rearranging Behavioral Consequences / Shared Activities	*149*
Chapter 10	Session 7: Dealing With Alcohol-Related Thoughts / Communication Part I	*163*
Chapter 11	Session 8: Drink Refusal / Communication Part II	*177*
Chapter 12	Session 9: Partner Role in Drink Refusal / Communication Part III / Relapse Prevention Part I	*189*

Chapter 13	Session 10: Problem Solving / Relapse Prevention Part II *203*
Chapter 14	Session 11: Relapse Prevention Part III / Acceptance Framework *217*
Chapter 15	Session 12: Review / Relapse Prevention Part IV *227*
	Drinking Patterns Questionnaire *233*
	References *263*
	About the Authors *271*

Chapter 1   *Introductory Information for Therapists*

Background Information and Purpose of This Program

This manual includes 12 therapy sessions, to be delivered in couple therapy modality, and covers (1) core cognitive-behavioral therapy (CBT) elements, including motivational enhancement, self-recording, functional analysis, self-management planning, and relapse prevention; (2) partner interventions, including functional analysis, modifying partner triggers, and modifying partner responses to drinking; and (3) couple interventions, including reciprocity enhancement and communication and problem solving. The session-by-session outline for this manual is shown in Table 1.1, found at the end of this chapter, with interventions broken down into categories of (1) routine interventions, (2) alcohol-specific coping skills interventions, (3) general coping skills interventions, (4) partner-related interventions, and (5) couple interventions.

The goals of the therapy are threefold: (1) to help the drinker stop drinking and maintain abstinence; (2) to help the partner change behaviors believed to contribute to continued drinking, such as behaviors that serve as triggers for drinking, positive responses that may reinforce drinking, and behaviors that protect the drinker from negative consequences of drinking; (3) to enhance the couple's relationship by increasing awareness of positive behaviors, increasing positive interactions, and improving their ability to communicate and solve problems. The treatment manual was designed and tested for clients with a goal of abstinence from alcohol; to date, there have not been any studies of adaptations of couple treatment models for clients who wish to moderate their drinking.

The therapy focuses more on drinking early in the therapy, and then gradually increases the focus on the interactional aspects of the treatment as the therapy progresses. The therapist, however, should maintain an interactional perspective throughout and focus on helping the couple learn to work together to deal with their problems.

Therapy involves both partners fully in each session. Although some interventions are directed toward individual behavior change for the drinker or the partner, the therapist should engage both partners in these individually oriented interventions. Involvement may include directing informational comments to each partner, asking each partner about his or her opinions about an intervention, or asking both partners for their perspectives about a particular behavior.

A challenge for therapists using the alcohol behavioral couple therapy (ABCT) model is balancing individual responsibility with an interactional perspective. The therapist should be explicit in stating that the drinker is responsible for his or her drinking and the partner is responsible for how she or he responds to the drinker. However, the therapist should also be explicit about noting ways that each partner can make behavior change easier or more difficult for the other and the ways that each partner triggers responses in the other (colloquially, "pushes each other's buttons"). The challenge is to enhance awareness of the circularity of interactions *and* acceptance of personal responsibility for change.

Alcohol Use Disorders

Alcohol use disorders (AUDs) are among the most common psychiatric diagnoses in the United States, with one-year prevalence estimates of 8.5% among adults (Grant et al., 2004). The health, economic, and social costs of AUDs are considerable. For example, estimated alcohol-related traffic fatalities in the United States were 16,919 (39.5% of all fatalities) in 2004 (Yi, Chen, & Williams, 2006); almost one in four violent offenders had been drinking at the time of the crime (U.S. Department of Health and Human Services, 2001); the economic costs of AUDs were estimated at $184.6 billion for 1998 (Harwood, 2000); and an estimated 50% of American adults have a family member with an AUD (U.S. Department of Health and Human Services, 2001).

It is common for persons with AUDs to have other psychological and social problems as well. A high percentage of those with AUDs experience other psychological problems that may be antecedent to, concurrent with, or consequent to their drinking (Rosenthal & Westreich, 1999). Other substance use disorders, depression, and anxiety disorders are most common and are found in as many as 60% of males in treatment. The most common Axis II disorder in men with an AUD is antisocial personality disorder, with rates ranging from 15% to 50%. Females are more likely than men to have mood disorders, and one quarter to a third of women with AUDs have a mood disorder prior to the onset of their alcoholism. The most common Axis II diagnosis among alcohol-dependent women is borderline personality disorder.

Cognitive deficits and medical problems are common among individuals with AUDs. These individuals may also have problems with employment, their interpersonal relationships, and the criminal justice system. Cognitive deficits in the areas of abstract reasoning, memory, and problem solving are most common (Bates, Bowden, & Barry, 2002). However, verbal functioning typically is unimpaired, so these cognitive problems are not immediately apparent. Heavy drinking may cause a variety of health problems in the cardiovascular, digestive, and neurological systems. Even without active medical problems, heavy drinking may result in nutritional deficits, poor energy, and a general feeling and appearance of poor health. Mortality rates are elevated for persons of all ages who have AUDs.

Interpersonal relationships also may be disrupted. The rates of separation and divorce are elevated, spousal violence is higher in both men and women with AUDs (Drapkin, McCrady, Swingle, & Epstein, 2005), and their spouses and children are more likely to have physical or emotional problems (Moos & Billings, 1982; Moos, Finney, & Gamble, 1982).

Involvement with the legal system also may complicate treatment because of charges related to driving while intoxicated (DWI), other alcohol-related offenses such as assault, or involvement with the child welfare system because of child abuse or neglect. Drug-related charges also may bring a client to treatment.

Knowledge about the efficacy of treatment for AUDs has increased substantially in the past 30 years. In an analysis of seven major, multisite treatment studies, Miller, Walters, and Bennett (2001) reported that, on average, 25% of clients maintained abstinence during the first year after treatment and 10% were drinking moderately and without problems. Mortality was less than 2%, the percentage of days that clients abstained from alcohol was 75%, and the amount that clients drank on drinking days decreased by 87%. Comparisons of treated and untreated alcohol-dependent community samples suggest that remission rates with treatment are higher than natural recovery rates (approximately 4.8% per year versus 3%) (Finney, Moos, & Timko, 1999). Comprehensive reviews of the efficacy of different treatment approaches suggest that there are good efficacy data for brief interventions, social skills training, the community reinforcement approach, behavioral contracting, behavioral couple therapy, case management, opiate antagonists such as naltrexone and nalmefene, and acamprosate (Miller & Wilbourne, 2002).

Given the complexity of AUDs, assessment is central to treatment planning and is an integral part of the treatment process described in this therapist guide. Chapter 3 provides a brief overview of the necessary components of assessment for the treatment.

Diagnostic Criteria for Alcohol Use Disorders (*DSM-IV-TR*, American Psychiatric Association, 2004)

Criteria for AUDs (alcohol abuse and alcohol dependence) are as follows:

Alcohol Abuse Criteria: *DSM-IV-TR*

A. A maladaptive pattern of substance use leading to clinically significant impairment or distress, as manifested by one (or more) or the following, occurring within a 12-month period:

    (1) Recurrent substance use resulting in a failure to fulfill major role obligations at work, school, or home (e.g., repeated absences or poor work performance related to substance use; substance-related absences, suspensions, or expulsions from school; neglect of children or household);

(2) Recurrent substance use in situations in which it is physically hazardous (e.g., driving an automobile or operating a machine when impaired by substance use);

(3) Recurrent substance-related legal problems (e.g., arrests for substance-related disorderly conduct);

(4) Continued substance use despite having persistent or recurrent social or interpersonal problems caused or exacerbated by the effects of the substance (e.g., arguments with spouse about consequences of intoxication, physical fights).

B. The symptoms have never met the criteria for Alcohol Dependence.

Alcohol Dependence Criteria: *DSM-IV-TR*

A. A maladaptive pattern of substance use, leading to clinically significant impairment or distress as manifested by three or more of the following occurring at any time in the same 12-month period:

(1) Tolerance, as defined by either of the following:
   (a) A need for markedly increased amounts of a substance to achieve intoxication or desired effect;
   (b) Markedly diminished effect with continued use of the same amount of the substance;

(2) Withdrawal, as manifested by either of the following:
   (a) the characteristic withdrawal syndrome for the substance, or
   (b) the same (or a closely related) substance is taken to relieve or avoid withdrawal symptoms;

(3) The substance is often taken in larger amounts or over a longer period than was intended;

(4) There is a persistent desire or unsuccessful efforts to cut down or control substance use;

(5) A great deal of time is spent in activities necessary to obtain the substance, use the substance, or recover from its effects;

(6) Important social, occupational, or recreational activities are given up or reduced because of substance use;

(7) The substance use is continued despite knowledge of having a persistent or recurrent physical or psychological problem that is likely to have been caused or exacerbated by the substance.

Specifiers:

- With physiological dependence: Evidence of tolerance or withdrawal (i.e., either Item 1 or 2 is present)

- Without physiological dependence: No evidence of tolerance or withdrawal (i.e., neither Item 1 nor 2 is present)

Development of This Treatment Program and Evidence Base

In the late 1960s/early 1970s, interactional perspectives began to be applied to psychological problems previously thought to be individually based, including AUDs (Steinglass, Weiner, & Mendelson, 1971). Research at the time suggested that involving the spouse in treatment resulted in better outcomes for the individual with an AUD (Hedberg & Campbell, 1974). Models for inpatient psychiatric treatment also were changing, with increasing interest in the role of the therapeutic milieu. McCrady and her colleagues (McCrady, Moreau, Paolino, & Longabaugh, 1982; McCrady, Paolino, Longabaugh, & Rossi, 1979) combined interactional and therapeutic milieu models in a randomized clinical trial of three treatments—joint hospital treatment for the drinker and spouse; couple therapy for the drinker and spouse during and after the drinker's hospitalization; and individual therapy for the drinker during and after the drinker's hospitalization—for 33 psychiatric hospital inpatients with AUDs. Nonparametric analyses suggested that the joint-admission and couples groups showed significant decreases in quantity of alcohol consumed, while decreases in the individual treatment condition were not significant (McCrady et al., 1979). In a 4-year follow-up of the participants, McCrady et al. (1982) reported that 6 of 18 joint-admission group participants were either continuously abstinent or had markedly improved throughout the 4 years; only 1 of 8 and 1 of 7 in each of the other two experimental groups showed comparable levels of improvement.

Based on the initial 6-month follow-up results, McCrady et al. (1979) concluded that the evidence did not support the expense and disruption associated with joint hospitalization but that the results suggested the value of spouse-involved treatment. Given that several other studies had found spouse involvement promising, McCrady then conducted a dismantling study, using a randomized clinical trial design to study the relative contributions of spouse presence, modifying spouse behaviors, and modifying the couple's relationship. In this study of 45 couples recruited through treatment programs and the community (McCrady et al., 1986; McCrady, Noel, Stout, Abrams, & Nelson, 1991), couples were randomly assigned to individual therapy with the spouse present; spouse-involved treatment that focused on changes in drinking and the spouse's ways of coping with the drinking; or a combination of individual, spouse, and couples therapy interventions. Over the 18 months of post-treatment follow-up, couples receiving the treatment that focused on the couple's relationship demonstrated better treatment retention, marital stability and satisfaction, less domestic violence, and better drinking outcomes.

Although our early results were promising, the majority of participants drank after treatment, so in a third clinical trial we tested alternate models for maintaining change after the couple therapy (ABCT) that had been most successful in the previous study; Dr. Epstein joined the research program in 1989. In the next study in the series, we treated 90 alcohol-dependent males and their spouses who were randomly assigned to ABCT or to ABCT combined with either enhanced relapse prevention (Marlatt & Gordon, 1985) interventions (RP/ABCT) or with referral to Alcoholics Anonymous (AA/ABCT). Participants were followed up for 18 months after treatment and they showed dramatic and statistically significant decreases in the frequency of their drinking through the 18-month follow-up period (McCrady, Epstein, & Hirsch, 1999; McCrady, Epstein, & Kahler, 2004). Drinking frequency among men in the study decreased from an average of 61% drinking days prior to treatment to drinking on approximately 20% of the days during follow-up. At 6 months following treatment, men in the combined RP/ABCT condition had shorter relapses than men in the other two treatment conditions; no between-group differences were evident at the 18-month follow-up.

Our research, and most other research on conjoint treatment models, had employed samples that were exclusively or largely male, so in the next study we decided to test the effectiveness of ABCT in a sample of women with alcohol dependence and their male partners. In this study, we randomized women to ABCT or alcohol behavioral individual therapy (ABIT) and followed up 102 alcohol-dependent females in committed relationships for 18 months after the baseline assessment (approximately 12 months after the 20-session treatment) (McCrady, Epstein, Cook, Jensen, & Hildebrandt, under review). Outcomes during and after treatment favored the ABCT condition (McCrady, Epstein, & Cook, 2003). We also found that ABCT seemed to attenuate the negative impact on drinking outcomes of Axis I psychopathology (McCrady et al., 2003). Despite the positive effects of ABCT for women who enrolled in the study, findings suggested possible limitations of conjoint models for women with AUDs not observed previously in male samples. First, a low percentage of women enrolled after their initial call about the study, and for 30% of those who did not enroll, factors related to the male partner played a primary role—he had an alcohol or drug problem, he was unwilling to participate, or the woman was unwilling to ask him to participate. We also found that some women randomized to ABCT had a strong preference for individual therapy, and they were more likely to drop out of the conjoint treatment (Morgan et al., unpublished paper). We also found that the male partners reported relatively low levels of engagement with the women's drinking (Green, Pugh, McCrady, & Epstein, in press).

Given the findings of our first clinical trial for women with AUDs, we are currently conducting another study with an all-female sample that builds on our previous findings. Women in the current clinical trial are allowed to choose whether or not treatment will involve their partner. We found that a substantial majority of women (98 of the first 115 women to enroll, or 83.7%) chose individual rather than conjoint treatment in the present study. We also found that the women choosing individual therapy were more likely than women choosing couple therapy to report that their male partners were heavier drinkers (McCrady, Epstein, & Cook, 2006). Participants in the couples arm of the study are being randomized to 12 sessions of ABCT, or a blend of ABCT and

ABIT, to test whether compliance and outcomes are improved when the women receive some individual attention and the male partners have to invest less in the treatment. This study is ongoing and no results are yet available.

Our research is part of a larger body of research on conjoint models for the conceptualization and treatment of alcohol and other substance use disorders. Results are fairly consistent across research groups in finding that conjoint models result in better drinking and drug outcomes and improved relationship functioning after treatment (see Fals-Stewart, O'Farrell, Birchler, Cordova, & Kelley, 2005 for a comprehensive review). Data also suggest that conjoint models of treatment for AUDs lead to greater decreases in intimate partner violence than individual treatment (O'Farrell, Murphy, Stephan, Fals-Stewart, & Murphy, 2004); that conjoint treatment is associated with improved functioning among the children (Kelley & Fals-Stewart, 2002); and that the treatments are cost-effective (O'Farrell et al., 1996).

Therapists for our studies all have had at least master's-level preparation and experience either in the treatment of AUDs or in CBT. Training has ranged from review of treatment manuals and weekly supervision to up to 16 hours of workshop training prior to seeing clients.

What is Alcohol Behavioral Couple Therapy (ABCT) for Alcohol Use Disorders?

Cognitive-Behavioral Treatment

This manual is based on a cognitive-behavioral approach to treatment. CBT derives from classical behavioral theories such as classical and operant conditioning and social modeling (see Carroll, 1999, for an in-depth discussion of CBT for substance use disorders). In CBT, we see substance use disorders as multiply determined, complex behaviors, but CBT approaches focus primarily on factors maintaining the alcohol use problems. Specifically, excessive drinking is treated as a habit, an over-learned behavior that can be unlearned. Classic CBT interventions are explicated in this manual and are organized around three major elements: motivational enhancement, functional analysis as a guiding framework for behavior change, and relapse prevention. CBT approaches to alcohol use problems have strong empirical support for their effectiveness (Carroll, 1999).

Motivational Enhancement

It is almost axiomatic that therapy cannot occur without a client, and a client with low motivation will not continue in treatment. The manual is structured to include several major approaches to enhancing and maintaining motivation:

1. **General therapeutic stance.** The therapist should treat the client with respect and as a person of value. Expressing interest in the client's emotional experiences and welfare, as well as the details of the client's daily life, is a part of valuing the client. The use of some motivational interviewing strategies (see Miller & Rollnick, 2002 for details) is appropriate, particularly reflective listening, empathy, and "rolling with resistance," but the therapy is skills based rather than motivationally based, so these basic therapeutic skills are combined with specific, structured aspects of the therapy.

2. **Feedback.** In the first session, the therapist provides feedback to the client about the extent and severity of his or her drinking. Such feedback has been demonstrated to enhance motivation to change (for example Miller, Sovereign, & Krege, 1988).

3. **Decisional matrix.** In Session 4, the therapist and client begin a decisional matrix exercise, which continues in later sessions. This exercise helps the client be more aware of the decision he or she has made to change and acknowledge the losses associated with stopping drinking, and enables the therapist to be empathic about the loss, as well as noting the potential gains from abstinence.

4. **Functional analysis.** In the functional analysis, the client examines the negative consequences of drinking in a variety of situations. This repeated focus on the reasons to stop also should reinforce the client's motivation to change.

Functional Analysis

The functional analysis is central to individualized CBT planning. Through the functional analysis and related exercises, the therapist and client identify situations that place the client at high risk for drinking, as well as the cognitive and affective responses that follow. Therapy then progresses by systematically helping the client learn ways to modify high-risk situations, learn different cognitive responses to the high-risk situations, learn new behaviors to use in response to high-risk situations, use insight about the positive consequences of drinking to learn new ways to obtain similar positive reinforcers through means other than drinking, and learn to focus on the negative consequences of drinking in high-risk situations. Specifics include the following:

1. **Identifying triggers/high-risk situations** is accomplished through interviewing, client recording of triggers on the daily self-recording cards, and through completion of the Drinking Patterns Questionnaire found in the appendix (DPQ, Zitter & McCrady, 1979). Worksheets help the client think of triggers in different areas of his or her life.

2. **Identifying dysfunctional thoughts** is accomplished primarily through careful interviewing, as well as completing specific behavior chains with the client. The therapist helps the client identify dysfunctional thoughts about self and others, as well as identifying positive expectancies about the effects that anticipated from drinking.

3. **Identifying dysfunctional emotions** also is accomplished primarily through careful interviewing, completing specific behavior chains with the client, as well as through the DPQ (Zitter & McCrady, 1979; Zweig, McCrady, & Epstein, 2008 see also Chapter 3).

4. **Identifying consequences of drinking** is accomplished through interviewing and completion of specific behavior chains. The therapist often has to help the client become more aware of the consequences, either positive or negative, of drinking in specific situations.

5. **Changing triggers.** From the list of triggers, the therapist then works with the client to develop strategies to change the most important triggers on the client's list of high-risk situations. Triggers that relate to environmental and habitual aspects of drinking are best handled through the self-management planning exercise.

6. **Changing thoughts and feelings.** The therapist needs to think carefully about the client's behavior chains to identify commonalities in the client's thinking about alcohol that can be addressed through specific interventions. Interventions targeted to changing thoughts and feelings include urge coping, dealing with alcohol-related thoughts, and, to some degree, the decisional matrix exercise described earlier under motivational enhancement.

7. **Changing behavior.** The therapist also needs to think carefully about specific behavior chains to identify coping skills that the client may lack. In CBT treatment, coping skills training focuses specifically on alcohol-related skills. These skills included drink refusal, anticipating high-risk situations, and problem solving.

8. **Changing consequences.** The functional analysis helps the client become aware of positive consequences from drinking and helps him or her identify alternative ways to obtain these same reinforcers.

Relapse Prevention

The treatment has drawn on several of Marlatt's original concepts of relapse prevention (Marlatt & Gordon, 1985), and the full course of treatment incorporates, in some respects, a relapse prevention approach as it focuses on identification and anticipation of high-risk situations and use of alternative coping skills. The last part of the treatment focuses more explicitly on relapse prevention, introducing the notion that clients do relapse and developing a set of strategies to both avoid relapses and cope with relapses that may occur.

Couple Treatment for Alcohol Use Problems

Rationale for Couple Treatment

ABCT is grounded in the assumption that drinking occurs in an interactional context, is maintained in part by interactions between the drinker and partner, and is changed most effectively by both changing the interactions between partners and by teaching each partner new individual coping skills. Throughout, the therapy maintains a dual focus on individual and interactional change. Partner behaviors and couple interactions are viewed as potential triggers for drinking. The partner's actions or the couple's interactions consequent to drinking may serve to reinforce the drinking, either by providing positive consequences for the drinking or by shielding the drinker from negative consequences of drinking that would otherwise occur. Epstein and McCrady (2002) provide a full explication of the ABCT model and therapists should be thoroughly familiar with that chapter.

Couple therapy has two unique aspects that reflect the assumption that drinking and relationship functioning are inextricably intertwined. First, the couple is helped to work together to deal with drinking-related issues, and partners are encouraged to support each other in coping more effectively with drinking triggers. Second, the therapy focuses heavily on enhancing the couple's relationship through improved communication and problem-solving skills as well as a focus on building more positive interactions between them. Couple interventions include the following:

Reciprocity Enhancement

The goal of reciprocity enhancement interventions is to increase positive exchanges between the partners so that they experience more pleasure in being with each other and, indirectly, so that the positive aspects of the relationship may serve as an incentive for the drinker to change and maintain change. Couples are first helped to identify positive behaviors from their partner and then learn to give each other feedback about these positive actions. Later, interventions focus on the development of shared enjoyable activities.

Communication and Problem Solving

These skills are taught through structured interventions designed to teach couples to identify positive and negative aspects of their communication and to then practice constructive communication skills. Problem-solving skills are introduced toward the end of treatment. The content used for communication skills training is individualized for each couple and often focuses on resentment and anger that have built up over the course of the relationship because of the drinking and the effects of the drinking on the partnership and the family. Thus, communication skills training helps repair the damage in an alcoholic relationship so that the couple can move on and change their relationship to one with abstinence, rather than drinking, as the base.

The couple therapy model also incorporates the partner into each of the following major aspects of CBT for AUDs:

Motivational Enhancement

Partners are helped to play several roles in enhancing motivation to change: (1) they may provide support and encouragement to continue in treatment when the drinker is reluctant to do so; (2) they contribute their perspective on pros and cons of drinking or abstinence to the development of a decisional matrix; (3) they are taught how to provide concrete and specific support/reinforcement for positive changes in drinking.

Functional Analysis

Partner behaviors and couple interactions are considered at each step in the functional analysis and treatment planning of couple therapy.

- **Identifying triggers.** The therapist helps the partner identify actions that may serve as triggers for drinking. These may include behaviors intended to influence the drinker to change (such as nagging), attempts to control the drinking or the drinker's behavior (such as restricting access to money), or the partner's own drinking.

- **Changing triggers.** The partner develops behavioral alternatives to actions that have been identified as triggers for drinking with the help of the therapist.

- **Changing consequences.** The therapist also helps the partner learn to provide positive reinforcement for positive behavior changes related to drinking, to decrease reinforcers for drinking, and to allow negative consequences to occur should the drinker drink.

Relapse Prevention

Relapse prevention is implemented in a couple's context. The couple thinks together about possible warning signs for relapse and develops relapse prevention and relapse management plans for each individual partner as well as the couple as a unit.

Risks and Benefits of This Treatment Program

The research base for ABCT points clearly to the potential benefits of the treatment—better drinking outcomes, improved relationship satisfaction, decreased domestic violence, and improved functioning for children in the home. There are two major risks in the ABCT approach. First, there is the potential for the couple's relationship to deteriorate and for them to ultimately separate or divorce. Persons with AUDs are at increased risk for separation and divorce, but it is possible that participation in couple therapy could accelerate the process if relationship issues become more apparent but cannot be resolved. Research data suggest the opposite—that the risk of separation and divorce is decreased with ABCT, but the therapist should be aware of the potential. Second, it can be difficult to engage couples in treatment together, particularly if the person with the AUD is a woman. As noted in the review of the evidence base for ABCT, male partners are more reluctant to participate in the treatment, and females with AUDs are more reluctant than males to have their male partner participate.

Alternative Treatments

There is good empirical evidence to support three outpatient approaches to treatment for persons with AUDs. Twelve-step facilitation counseling (TSF) uses counseling procedures to help a client become integrated with AA, and research suggests that clients who participate in TSF have a greater likelihood of maintaining complete abstinence from alcohol than clients receiving other forms of outpatient counseling (Project MATCH Research Group, 1997a). Additionally, clients whose social network strongly encourages them to drink do particularly well with TSF (Longabaugh, Wirtz, Zweben, & Stout, 1998). Motivational enhancement therapy (MET) uses motivational techniques to help clients recognize their drinking problems and develop the motivation to change (Miller, Zweben, DiClemente, & Rychtarik, 1994). MET appears to be particularly effective with clients who enter treatment angry and resentful of the treatment process (Project MATCH Research Group, 1997b). CBT helps clients identify high-risk situations for drinking and develop cognitive, affective, and behavioral skills to cope with these situations (Kadden et al., 1995). CBT appears to be particularly effective with clients who are lower in the severity of their alcohol dependence (Project MATCH Research Group, 1997a) and is the only treatment model designed to accommodate clients whose goals are to moderate their drinking rather than to abstain (Hester, 2003). More recently, aspects of all three treatments have been combined into one treatment package (Miller, 2004), but research evidence for the combined approach is limited.

There are three medications with evidence supporting their use in the treatment of AUDs. Disulfiram (Antabuse®) blocks the metabolic breakdown of alcohol, leading the patient to become ill if he drinks while on the medication (Barber & O'Brien, 1999). Naltrexone (Revia®) is an opiate antagonist that appears to help clients who experience strong cravings to drink; evidence suggests that naltrexone results in less drinking among patients who relapse (O'Malley et al.,

1992; Volpicelli, Alterman, Hayashida, & O'Brien, 1992). In a series of European trials (Paille et al., 1995), acamprosate (Campral®) appeared to increase the probability that patients would maintain complete abstinence while on the medication. Findings from a recent U.S. trial did not support the effectiveness of acamprosate (Anton et al., 2006).

The Role of Medications

In our research, approximately one-third of female clients entering the clinical trial have been taking medications, primarily antidepressants, for other Axis I disorders (Epstein, McCrady, Drapkin, & Cook, 2005). Some clients have been referred for antidepressant medication during treatment. There are no contraindications to using these medications in combination with ABCT, but there are no controlled trials comparing ABCT with and without antidepressants.

O'Farrell's approach to ABCT includes a daily Antabuse contract that specifies that the person with the AUD will take the Antabuse tablet in front of his or her partner, and they each state the positive reasons for using the medication in this way (O'Farrell, 1993). In one component analysis of his approach to ABCT, O'Farrell and his colleagues (O'Farrell, Choquette, & Cutter, 1998) reported a strong concurrent association between use of the Antabuse contract and positive drinking outcomes. No studies have tested the relative effectiveness of ABCT versus pharmacotherapy, and no studies have examined the effectiveness of ABCT in combination with either naltrexone or acamprosate.

Outline of This Treatment Program

Each session follows the same format of 90 min, to be roughly divided into three segments. First, do the routine interventions in every session: check in, review homework, and graph daily monitoring data. Then, present the rationale for and then practice in session one or two new skills. Use the worksheets for working in session and for assignments of completion of work started in session. Use the handouts to reinforce the material covered in session and as homework assignments.

For the last 10 min of the session, assign homework for the week and review and plan strategies for upcoming high-risk drinking situations. A session-by-session outline of the manual is provided in Table 1.1. If sessions of 50–60 min are necessary, the clinician can retain the basic format of interventions and topics both within and across sessions but can cover fewer topics in each session and extend the length of treatment. Alternatively, the clinician may select which interventions are most relevant and important for each couple and retain the 12-session length of treatment.

Use of the Client Workbook

The client workbook is designed to be used in conjunction with each therapy session. The workbook is organized into chapters that correspond to each of the 12 therapy sessions and includes a summary of the major concepts introduced in the session. The workbook includes worksheets that the therapist should complete with the client during the session and also additional worksheets for homework assignments between sessions. Instruct clients to bring the workbook to each therapy session. Therapists are advised to have extra, loose copies of the in-session worksheets to use with clients who forget the workbook for a particular session. The workbook also includes a place to graph the client's weekly drinking and drinking urges, and the therapist should update the graph each week during the session to provide immediate feedback to the client on his or her progress.

Table 1.1 Outline of Alcohol Behavioral Couple Therapy

Routine Interventions	Alcohol-Related Skills Interventions	Partner-Related Alcohol Interventions	General Coping Skills	Couple Therapy

Session 1—Introduction / Rationale / Self-Recording

A. BAL	E. Feedback from baseline and clinical screen 20 ⊕	F. Enhancing partner motivation to participate 10 ⊕		
B. Opening statements; building rapport 10 ⊕	H. Introduction to self-recording 10 ⊕	G. Partner support for client's change 10 ⊕		
C. Treatment rationale 10 ⊕	I. Abstinence Plan -*optional and/or* 5 ⊕			
D. Treatment requirements 5 ⊕	Possible problem areas -*optional*			
K. Homework 5 ⊕	J. Anticipating high-risk situations 5 ⊕			

Session 2—Functional Analysis / Noticing Positive Behavior

A. BAL	E. Functional analysis 35 ⊕			F. Noticing positive behaviors in each other ("Notice something nice") 20 ⊕
B. Overview of session 5 ⊕	G. Anticipating high-risk situations 10 ⊕			
C. Review self-recording and homework 5 ⊕				
D. Check in 10 ⊕				
H. Homework 5 ⊕				

continued

Table 1.1 Outline of Alcohol Behavioral Couple Therapy *continued*

Routine Interventions	Alcohol-Related Skills Interventions	Partner-Related Alcohol Interventions	General Coping Skills	Couple Therapy

Session 3—High-Risk Hierarchy / Partner Functional Analysis Part I / Self-Management Plans

A. BAL
B. Overview of session 5 ⊕
C. Review self-recording and homework 10 ⊕
D. Check in 5 ⊕
J. Homework 5 ⊕

F. Developing a hierarchy of high-risk situations 15 ⊕
H. Self-management plans 20 ⊕
I. Anticipating high-risk situations 5 ⊕

G. Partner-related functional analysis 20 ⊕

E. Continue with "Notice something nice" 5 ⊕

Session 4—Partner Functional Analysis Part II / Enhancing Motivation to Change

A. BAL
B. Overview of session 5 ⊕
C. Review self-recording and homework 5 ⊕
D. Check in 5 ⊕
J. Homework 5 ⊕

G. Continuation of self-management plans, including Alcohol in the House plan 20 ⊕
H. Decisional matrix and motivation enhancement 20 ⊕
I. Anticipating high-risk situations 5 ⊕

F. Complete functional analysis of partner-related patterns 20 ⊕

E. "Notice something nice" and feedback 5 ⊕

continued

Routine Interventions	Alcohol-Related Skills Interventions	Partner-Related Alcohol Interventions	General Coping Skills	Couple Therapy

Session 5—Dealing With Urges / Decreasing Partner Triggers

A. BAL
B. Overview of session 2 ⏱
C. Review self-recording and homework 5 ⏱
D. Check in 10 ⏱
J. Homework 3 ⏱

E. Dealing with urges 15 ⏱
H. Review of skills and progress thus far 20 ⏱
I. Anticipating high-risk situations 5 ⏱

F. Partner role in dealing with urges 10 ⏱
G. Decreasing partner triggers for drinking 20 ⏱

Session 6—Rearranging Behavioral Consequences / Shared Activities

A. BAL
B. Overview of session 5 ⏱
C. Review self-recording and homework 10 ⏱
D. Check in 5 ⏱
I. Homework 5 ⏱

E. Rearranging behavioral consequences 30 ⏱
H. Anticipating high-risk situations 5 ⏱

G. Partner-changing consequences—Decreasing protection 15 ⏱

F. Shared activities 15 ⏱

Session 7—Dealing With Alcohol-Related Thoughts / Communication Part I

A. BAL
B. Overview of session 5 ⏱
C. Review self-recording and homework 5 ⏱

F. Dealing with alcohol-related thoughts 25 ⏱
H. Anticipating high-risk situations 3 ⏱

E. Shared activities plan for next few weeks 10 ⏱

continued

21

Table 1.1 Outline of Alcohol Behavioral Couple Therapy *continued*

Routine Interventions	Alcohol-Related Skills Interventions	Partner-Related Alcohol Interventions	General Coping Skills	Couple Therapy
D. Check in 5 ⊕ I. Homework 2 ⊕				G. Introduction to communication training 35 ⊕

Session 8—Drink Refusal / Communication Part II

Routine Interventions	Alcohol-Related Skills Interventions	Partner-Related Alcohol Interventions	General Coping Skills	Couple Therapy
A. BAL B. Overview of session 5 ⊕ C. Review self-recording and homework 10 ⊕ D. Check in 5 ⊕ I. Homework 5 ⊕	F. Drink refusal training 25 ⊕ H. Anticipating high-risk situations 5 ⊕			E. Extending shared activity 10 ⊕ G. Communication skills 25 ⊕

Session 9—Partner Role in Drink Refusal / Communication Part III / Relapse Prevention Part I

Routine Interventions	Alcohol-Related Skills Interventions	Partner-Related Alcohol Interventions	General Coping Skills	Couple Therapy
A. BAL B. Overview of session 5 ⊕ C. Review self-recording and homework 5 ⊕ D. Check in 5 ⊕ I. Homework 5 ⊕	G. Seemingly irrelevant decisions 35 ⊕ H. Anticipating high-risk situations 5 ⊕	E. Partner role in drink situations & in drink refusal 15 ⊕		F. Communication skills: leveling and editing 15 ⊕

continued

Routine Interventions	Alcohol-Related Skills Interventions	Partner-Related Alcohol Interventions	General Coping Skills	Couple Therapy

Session 10—Problem Solving / Relapse Prevention Part II

A. BAL
B. Overview of session 5 ⏱
C. Review self-recording and homework 5 ⏱
D. Check in 5 ⏱
I. Homework 5 ⏱

G. Relapse Prevention II: Identifying & managing warning signs of relapse (including partner role) 20 ⏱

H. Anticipating high-risk situations 5 ⏱

E. Problem solving as a general coping skill 20 ⏱

F. Joint problem solving 25 ⏱

Session 11—Relapse Prevention Part III / Acceptance Framework

A. BAL
B. Overview of session 5 ⏱
C. Review self-recording and homework 5 ⏱
D. Check in 5 ⏱
I. Homework 5 ⏱

E. Handling slips and relapses 35 ⏱
H. Anticipating high-risk situations 5 ⏱

F. Partner role in handling slips & relapses 10 ⏱

G. Acceptance/ Change framework 20 ⏱

continued

23

Table 1.1 Outline of Alcohol Behavioral Couple Therapy *continued*

Routine Interventions	Alcohol-Related Skills Interventions	Partner-Related Alcohol Interventions	General Coping Skills	Couple Therapy

Session 12—Review / Relapse Prevention Part IV

A. BAL	E. Review of techniques & planning for maintenance: Final review & maintenance planning	40 ⊕		
B. Overview of session 5 ⊕				
C. Review self-recording and homework 5 ⊕	F. Developing a relapse contract	25 ⊕		
D. Check in 5 ⊕				
G. Follow-up contract 5 ⊕				

24

Chapter 2

Clinical Issues in Alcohol Behavioral Couple Therapy (ABCT)

Managing the Couples Sessions

From the beginning of couples work, it is important to set the stage with some basic rules of the sessions. In this way, you can begin to help the couple with their communication skills, establish yourself as the manager of the session, and help prevent episodes of overt anger and argument that might derail the therapy. Couples often are quite angry at one another by the time they attend treatment, so the therapist should expect anger, blaming, resistance, and sadness.

As therapy progresses, some expressions of anger are unavoidable and even desirable. However, repeatedly using sessions as a forum for airing grievances will prevent progress and may lead to early termination of couple treatment by one partner or the other. You must carefully monitor the type and amount of marital conflict in the session and consciously decide when to let it continue and when and how to step in and redirect. In other words, relationship conflict is natural, expected, and has a useful place in conjoint therapy. However, you must be in control of the session at all times, and expressions of conflict are at your discretion. If conflict is intense and escalates to the point where you feel the session has gotten out of control, it is time to model a "time out." You may say something like, *"This arguing is getting too intense now and isn't helpful. It looks like we need to take 5 minutes to calm down, so let's take a break, take a little walk one at a time, and then re-connect."* Before ending such a session, take 5–10 min at the end of the session to debrief the couple, reflect on what has happened in the session, and predict that one or both partners may want to continue the argument in the car on the way home or during the week between sessions. It is important to highlight the lack of benefits of continuing to argue. You may direct the couple by saying, *"Continuing this argument in the car would be an exercise in frustration for both of you. You're not ready to talk about this together without a third party there. I suggest you really make the effort to let this rest for now, even if it means not talking to each other on the way home. We can talk about it together next time."*

Following are some tips and strategies for managing a session in which the couple is angry and arguing.

- Lay the ground rules at the beginning of therapy so the couple can expect you to step in at any time.

- Use nonverbal behavior to help manage the session (e.g., hold up your hands to signal "stop"; lean forward into the couple and begin talking).

- Feel free to interrupt the arguing.

- If the couple begins to argue again, just hold up a hand and guide the couple to use more productive communication skills.

- Do not refer to either partner in the room as "he" or "she"—you should always use their names.

- If one partner is complaining about the other partner to you, it is usually appropriate (especially after initial assessment and rapport-building sessions) to redirect his or her comments directly to the partner.

Continued Drinking

At the initial intake, the client answers a written "drinking goal" question, for instance, that he or she has decided to remain abstinent forever, or wants to have a drink occasionally, or has some other drinking goal (see Chapter 3). Despite this question, it is important to make it clear to the client at the initial intake interview that this is an abstinence-based program and that you are asking the client to commit to trying to become abstinent. If the client is unwilling to make a commitment to strive for abstinence during the 3-month treatment period, we typically have excluded the client from the clinical trial and provided an appropriate clinical referral. We don't expect each client to become abstinent right away; in fact, we work with each client individually to create abstinence plans starting in Session 1. This manual is geared toward achieving abstinence by Session 5. Therapists in clinical practice may take a different approach to clients with non-abstinent goals (see, for example, Hester, 2003), but ABCT has been tested using the approach described here.

You should be aware of the client's answer to the drinking goal question and should take the client's level of ambivalence about abstinence into account when devising the abstinence plan in Session 1. Some clients continue to drink through a number of sessions. If the client continues to drink past Session 5, it is important to address this issue and to explore the continued drinking until both you and the client understand why it is still occurring. At each session up to Session 5, you should review the abstinence plan and revise it if the client is not making progress toward his or her quit date. In all cases, if a client is continuing to drink by Session 5 we suggest a case review with a colleague or clinical supervisor. Some of the most common reasons clients continue to drink are listed here with suggested interventions.

Inability to Follow the Plan

The client is struggling with the drinking reduction plan and is unable to follow it; he or she may reduce the level of drinking to some degree but not substantially. In other words, the client is not really getting better despite genuine efforts. In this case, by Session 5 it may be time to consider the need for a higher level of care, such as an intensive outpatient or inpatient treatment, or an alternative, more definitive means to stopping drinking, such as a detoxification program.

Change of Mind

The client has reconsidered the commitment to abstinence during treatment and informs you that he or she no longer intends to work toward complete abstinence. In this case, you may decide to continue to use ABCT with a goal of moderated drinking, may decide to refer the couple to a therapist with expertise in moderation approaches (if you do not have this expertise), or may decide to try to encourage the client to reconsider a moderated drinking goal. It is usually best not to directly confront the client about his or her desire to continue drinking. Rather, use a motivational interviewing style. Revisit the decisional matrix to try to help the client remember the negative consequences of drinking that led to the initial decision to seek help, and use motivational interviewing techniques to help the client explore ambivalence about abstinence in an effort to enhance a commitment to be abstinent for the treatment duration. You may also engage the partner in the discussion of drinking goals, although there is a danger that the partner will express strong opinions or make specific demands that elicit a negative reaction from the client. Some comments that may be helpful in addressing ambivalence are as follows:

> *It's very common for people to have mixed feelings about abstinence, and many people who come to treatment for alcohol problems say that they would like to have a drink now and then, or do 'controlled drinking' or 'social drinking.' This program is abstinence-based, and while I haven't asked you to commit to remaining abstinent your whole life, I do ask that you make a commitment to be abstinent during the 3 months you're in treatment. I'd like you to have a stretch of time with alcohol out of your life so that you can get used to it a bit, and see what it's like. Often people don't realize how much alcohol plays a role in their lives until it's gone for a while, and they don't realize how much better they feel without alcohol until they've gotten used to living without it. While you're in this program, you might as well take advantage of the time to learn the skills to be abstinent, so that you will always have those skills should you want to use them.*
>
> *The second reason this is an abstinence-based program is that abstinence is the safest choice. You won't have alcohol-related problems if you're not drinking. And it's too easy to start out with a drink here and there and then work your way up over time to problem drinking again.*

At this point, you can review the client's relapse history.

> *Third, 'controlled drinking' is not the same as 'social drinking.' Social drinkers can have a drink here and there, but they don't think about drinking otherwise. They can take it or leave it. Controlled or "moderated" drinking means continuing to keep alcohol in your life, but always working to control it, count drinks, not lose self-control, and be aware and deliberate about your drinking. Moderated drinking means limiting your drinking to a certain number of drinks per week and per drinking occasion and requires that you spend quite a bit of energy thinking about alcohol in order to keep your drinking contained. For many people, it turns out that abstinence is easier in the long run than 'controlled drinking,' which requires a whole different focus in treatment and in your life. What are your thoughts?*

Ambivalence

The client voices commitment to abstinence but continues to drink at reduced levels and is clearly ambivalent about stopping drinking completely. In this case, you can use some of the strategies just discussed for the client who has changed his or her mind or you can keep working toward the abstinence goal without really directly addressing the choice of moderated drinking. For instance, while graphing the client's drinking patterns, you can remind the client that x number of weeks are left in therapy and it is desirable for him or her to have some weeks of sobriety while still in treatment to discuss with his or her partner (and you) how abstinence feels. As this process is ongoing, use a motivational interviewing style in therapy sessions to highlight ambivalence and positive reasons to stop drinking. Or, frame the client's drinking pattern as an initial drastic reduction (which is common) and then a plateau, which also is common, and then let the client know that he or she needs to work toward the next plateau and the next, until the drinking is at 0. Thus, after the initial reduction, drinking during subsequent weeks can be treated as relapses, or slips, in the process of attaining abstinence.

Domestic Violence

If domestic violence is present in the relationship, immediately assess the current severity/frequency and make a referral for treatment if necessary. Consultation with a peer or supervisor also is advisable. You should also do the following:

- Determine if there are weapons in the home. Make a plan to get them out of the home or render them unusable.

- Identify interactional sequences leading up to violent episodes. Problem solve with the couple to help each partner modify his or her role in the sequences. Work on relevant communication skills.

- Emphasize that it is the responsibility of the person who has the impulse to be violent to refrain from violent behavior, but it is the responsibility of the abused partner to keep him- or herself safe by not provoking the abuser and by creating an individualized safety plan.

- Discuss legal options such as a restraining order.

- Identify a safe place for the abused partner to go.

- Give the abused partner phone numbers for shelters and hotlines.

- Help the abused partner plan how to save money and if necessary, prepare for a quick departure by having a packed bag ready.

- Identify barriers to leaving the home and problem solve.

Child Abuse or Neglect

If a client makes reference to child abuse or neglect, you need to assess the situation further. Ask specific questions of the client and the spouse/partner that will provide a clearer view of the nature of the abuse or neglect. Examples of possible questions are, *"When you hit your child, do you use your hand or an object?"*; *"Do you leave marks when you hit your child?"*; *"For how long a time do you leave your child unsupervised?"*

We are legally bound to report cases of suspected child abuse or neglect, and the informed consent for treatment should indicate this limitation on confidentiality. If the situation is unclear, bring it up immediately with a peer consultant or supervisor to get feedback on the next steps to take. Typically, our procedure is to discuss the situation with the client to inform him or her that we are legally obligated to report the incident to the state's child protective services (CPS) unit and that the first step CPS will take will be to investigate the need for further action on their part. We inform the clients that our goal is to work with them to ensure that their children are safe. Be sure that you have contact information for your state's CPS.

Arrival to Treatment With Elevated BAL

At the beginning of each session, the client and the partner both are given a Breathalyzer to determine the presence of alcohol in their systems. Do not proceed if BAL of either partner is .05 or greater. There may be instances when the client has a positive alcohol screen but adamantly denies being under the influence. No matter what the client says, nothing but alcohol will result in an actual blood alcohol level (BAL) of .01 or more, although smoking a cigarette or using mouthwash within 15 min of the breath test can result in a spurious reading. However, if the BAL still is positive after 15 min then you can rule out these proximal causes.

In any case where you have to terminate the session early because of an elevated BAL, you must determine an immediate plan to assure the safety of the client, determine whether the pattern of drinking prior to the session warrants a higher level of care, and develop a short-term plan. If it seems appropriate for the couple to continue in conjoint outpatient treatment, schedule another session as soon as is feasible.

Do not engage the client or partner in confrontational interchanges around the use, or non-use, of alcohol. Simply inform the individual with the elevated BAL that there is alcohol in his or her system currently above the .05 level, that your policy is to reschedule the session, and that you do not make any exceptions to this policy. If the BAL is a bit over .05, it is worth waiting for 15–20 min to re-take a Breathalyzer reading to see if the BAL is on the descending limb (i.e. going down). If it decreases to below .05, you can hold the session.

If the client or partner's BAL is above the legal driving limit (.08), arrangements for getting home safely need to be made. If the driver is the one with the elevated BAL, the couple can wait in your office until the driver's BAL is below the legal driving limit, *if* his or her BAL is on the descending limb and is close enough to the limit. Or, the sober partner can drive the couple home or to work, and if they came in separate cars they can return later to retrieve the intoxicated partner's car. If the intoxicated individual refuses to wait or call for alternative transportation, our general policy is to inform him or her that we must call the police to let them know that an intoxicated person is leaving the building and is planning to drive. Check with a local attorney to determine best practices in your own state.

If the client or partner's BAL is high enough to potentially be dangerous (.40 and above, roughly) there are additional considerations. At these levels, alcohol poisoning can occur, and the individual will need medical attention. The safest option is to have the sober partner take the other to the nearest emergency room (ER). If this is impossible, the couple can arrange for a taxi to the nearest ER and arrange to have a friend or family member come pick up the car, or one of the partners can take a taxi back to the therapist's office to get the car later.

In some cases, if the client agrees to go directly to a detoxification or inpatient rehabilitation unit, the therapist can help the couple contact their insurance company to determine which facilities are in the client's network and to get pre-authorization for admission. Then, arrangements will need to be made to transport the client to the treatment facility. Some treatment facilities provide pick-up services.

Difficulties in Developing a Therapeutic Alliance

In treatment, there are times when the therapist has difficulty connecting with a specific client or partner. Additionally, there are times when clients or partners will have a negative, hostile attitude toward their therapist. When this occurs, attrition is common. In other instances, the couple will remain in treatment but express their negative and hostile attitude. When faced with this attitude, it is common for therapists to feel frustrated, angry, and unsure of themselves. If you run into this problem, it is important that you do not react with anger or act defensively. Instead, adopt the motivational interviewing style of "rolling with the resistance," listening reflectively, and responding empathically. Genuinely attempt to understand the client's negativity and what "kernel of truth" the client is responding to (*do you* have a negative attitude toward the client?). Openly addressing problems in the therapeutic relationship often will be enough to resolve it satisfactorily. However, if there are continued strains in the therapy alliance, bring this up with a peer consultant or supervisor for feedback and suggestions, and consider referral to another therapist.

Homework

Compliance with homework requirements is a marker of motivation, good rapport with the therapist, effort to practice skills learned in session, and treatment retention and positive treatment outcome. Homework is an important and unique aspect of CBT and is especially important in helping drinkers and partners practice and consolidate skills discussed in session to make successful changes.

Highlight the importance of homework explicitly by reviewing the rationale for it. You may say something like the following:

> *I only have you for 1 1/2 hours per week—the rest of your life has you for the other 166 1/2! For us to make progress, it's important that you take what we discuss in here and apply it during the week. Changing a habit is hard work, and that's where the homework comes in. If you hang in there and keep trying, eventually it will work and it will also become easier.*

Highlight the importance of homework implicitly by always remembering to review assigned and completed homework carefully and in a clinically meaningful way so that the couple feels reinforced for completing their homework and also so that they understand how it can be meaningful for them.

Homework Non-compliance

Address the issue of homework non-completion directly by commenting that you notice that the client or partner doesn't seem to like doing at-home assignments and you're wondering what's behind that. Use reflective listening and a motivational interviewing style to try to understand and help the client or partner understand his or her ambivalence about doing homework.

Be aware that not completing homework may be indicative of a deeper ambivalence toward therapy, stopping drinking, or the couple's relationship. Begin to explore this from a position of concern for the client's anxiety about giving up drinking, of desiring to understand his or her experience of the therapy, and of acknowledging that changes often are unsettling to an intimate relationship. Not addressing homework non-compliance can result in therapy attrition.

Some people have personalities or hectic life contexts that make it difficult to complete homework. For instance, impulsive, nonverbal, action-oriented people often find it difficult to focus and complete CBT homework. These people can be told that one of the points of CBT and also CBT homework is in fact to help the client "slow down the process of automatic behavior, or habits" so that they become easier to identify and control. Thus, though especially difficult for them, these clients need to make the extra effort to try to complete the homework as best as they can to get the most out of therapy.

Some people say, "When I do the homework it just reminds me of drinking and is a trigger for me. It's easier for me to stay sober if I just don't think about it." For these people it's important to tell them that if thinking about homework is still a trigger for them it may indicate that they still need to work on their abstinence coping skills. Suggest to the client that he or she might want to try to do the homework and get through the associated cravings to further consolidate his or her abstinence and to acquire new skills the client may want to use one day.

Some couples find it difficult to complete joint assignments because of anger or disappointment with the partner, lack of effective communication or problem-solving skills, or schedules that allow little time together. The therapist should identify the sources of difficulty with joint homework as a first step.

Presence of an Axis I Disorder

Many clients with AUDs show signs of an Axis I disorder (mood, anxiety, eating disorders, etc.). It is important to be familiar with the *DSM-IV* criteria for Axis I clinical syndromes so that you can assess the severity of the problem and refer for additional treatment if necessary. During the assessment (see Chapter 3), the therapist should use some structured means to assess for Axis I disorders.

In assessing the severity of the Axis I disorder, include the following:

Assess suicidality. If a client is suicidal, discuss your concerns and options with the client. When assessing suicidality, you should assess thoughts, means, plans, and history of attempts. If the client presents as a suicide risk, you may have to ensure that he or she is evaluated at a psychiatric emergency service. Or, you may call the police to have them come to help you to transport the client to a local emergency room.

Explain to clients that many symptoms of depression and anxiety will diminish once they achieve and maintain sobriety for several weeks. Monitor the level of depression and anxiety over the course of treatment. In the first month of abstinence, it is common for clients to experience anxious and depressed feelings. If these persist for longer than a month post-abstinence, concerns and questions should be brought to clinical supervision. When indicated, the therapist should make appropriate clinical referrals. These might include referrals to mental heath counseling and/or a psychiatric assessment for medication.

Presence of an Axis II Disorder

Many of our clients meet criteria for an Axis II disorder. In populations with substance use disorders, antisocial personality and borderline personality disorders are the most common Axis II diagnoses. Most often, individuals with Axis II disorders do not perceive the need for their behavior to change and are not receptive to referrals for psychiatric treatment. Clear structure and consistent adherence to boundaries is important for the therapist when working with individuals with Axis II disorders. Therapists should use peer consultation or supervision as a way to get feedback on using various interventions as well as to discuss their own reactions to working with individuals with Axis II disorders.

Need for Additional Services or Higher Level of Care

Reasons for additional or more intensive treatment might be continued heavy drinking, lack of progress toward an abstinence goal, increased drug use, depression, or simply a desire to attend additional treatment and get more support for abstinence. Consult with your colleagues if necessary, and maintain a list of referrals for treatments at higher levels of care.

Chapter 3 Assessing Alcohol Use and Problems

Materials Needed

- Breathalyzer or other alcohol breath test (to test both partners)
- Clinical Intake Semi-Structured Interview Form
- Semi-Structured Clinical Interview for *DSM-IV-TR* Axis I Diagnoses (SCID-I) Alcohol and Drug Sections
- Form-90 (for client)
- Timeline Followback Interview (for client)
- Personal Drinking Goal form (for client)
- Short Inventory of Problems (SIP) or Drinker's Inventory of Consequences (DrInC) (for client)
- Beck Depression Inventory (for client)
- Beck Anxiety Inventory (for client)
- Dyadic Adjustment Scale (for both client and partner)
- Areas of Change Questionnaire (for both client and partner)
- Modified Conflict Tactics Scale (for both client and partner)
- Coping Questionnaire (for partner)
- Quantity Frequency Index (for partner)

Outline

- Conduct a semi-structured clinical intake interview with the couple

- Have client and partner complete self-report questionnaires

- Interpret assessment data to establish diagnosis, severity of problem, and level of care determination

- Provide feedback to couple regarding recommendations for treatment

Overview of Assessment

This chapter provides an assessment protocol for use with couples, including both semi-structured clinical interviews and self-report measures.

For the client, the assessment data will yield screening, diagnostic, and severity information for the alcohol use, as well as the history and consequences of the alcohol use, quantity/frequency and drinking pattern, typical and peak levels of blood alcohol level, level of care determination, level of motivation to change drinking behavior, and associated psychiatric problems.

For the spouse or partner, the assessment yields information on strategies used to cope with the client's drinking, and her own quantity and frequency of alcohol consumption.

For the couple, the assessment provides information on relationship functioning and happiness, relationship content areas that each partner would like to change, and strategies for resolving conflict (including violence).

The chapter first briefly reviews areas of assessment that are important, and then guides you through administration of the battery, as well as interpretation of results.

The assessment has four purposes: The data are used (1) as an overall evaluation of problems to determine appropriate level of care and services need; (2) to help with abstinence planning; (3) as the basis for treatment interventions such as motivational enhancement and functional analysis; and (4) to generate feedback to enhance motivation. Feedback regarding the assessment data collected is given to the couple in Session 1. Session 1 of this therapist manual provides information necessary to calculate BAL and interpret quantity of alcohol use vis-à-vis normative data, to allow for interpretation of the assessment data. In the CBT model, continued assessment and a feedback loop throughout treatment are important aspects of the treatment. These are accomplished through daily drinking and relationship functioning logs completed by clients throughout the program that are reviewed each week at the start of the session. These monitoring forms are presented in Session 1. Assessment to complete a functional analysis of the client's drinking occurs as part of the treatment itself and is accomplished in the first two to three sessions.

Assessment Plan

Assessment typically requires one to three sessions, depending on the severity of the alcohol problem, complications such as comorbid psychopathology and/or drug use, and marital functioning. If possible, allot 90–120 min for the first assessment session so that much of the assessment can be done in this one extended session.

In this treatment model, assessment is considered part of the therapy protocol; both partners attend the assessment sessions, and it is important to keep in mind that this may be the first time the drinker is speaking candidly, or speaking at all about the alcohol use, in front of his significant other. The assessment sessions are thus often quite difficult and emotional for both partners, and it is important for you to establish rapport with each one and to communicate accurate empathy with each perspective, while moving the interviews forward and gathering all necessary information. Table 3.1 lists topics to cover in the initial clinical interview with both partners present. Each aspect of the table will then be described (see McCrady, 2007, for more detail).

Table 3.1 Topics to Cover in Initial Assessment (both partners present)

1. Initial orientation
    a. Introductions
    b. Breath alcohol test
    c. Brief questionnaires
2. Initial assessment
    a. Presenting problems
    b. Role of alcohol in presenting problems
    c. Other concerns
    d. How drinking has affected the partner
    e. How drinking has affected the relationship
3. Drinking/drug-use assessment
    a. Client
        i. Last alcohol consumption
        ii. Length of drinking/drug-use problem
        iii. Quantity, frequency, pattern of drinking
        iv. Negative consequences of drinking/drug-use problem
        v. DSM-IV-TR Symptoms
        vi. Assessment of need for detoxification
    b. Partner
        i. Quantity, frequency, pattern of drinking
4. Assessment of other problems
    a. Psychotic symptoms
    b. Depression
    c. Anxiety
    d. Cognitive impairment
    e. Health status
    f. Medications
    g. Other drug use
5. Assessment of domestic violence
    a. Review of Modified Conflict Tactics Scale

Initial Orientation: Introductions, Breath Alcohol Test, Brief Questionnaires

Establishing Rapport

You should spend a few minutes establishing general rapport to help the couple feel comfortable through small talk. Then describe what will happen in the intake by saying something like the following:

In the initial 1–3 sessions, I'll be asking you lots of questions, and you'll fill out some questionnaires. I'll give you feedback about whether or not I think this treatment is the best choice for you at this time. Please ask me as many questions as you want.

Breath Alcohol Test

During the intake, and at the start of all subsequent sessions, you will test both the client's and his partner's BAL using a Breathalyzer. You can purchase a handheld Breathalyzer from any of several companies online, such as Alcopro.com. There are other methods to test BAL on site, such as saliva sticks and other types of single-wrapped devices for saliva, urine, and breath testing.

Introduce the breath test as follows:

My policy to is to use a Breathalyzer to check for alcohol in your system for both of you, even though I understand that it is (name of drinking partner) *who is coming for treatment of the alcohol problem. It is important to have a clear head during our meetings together. This means you should not drink alcohol or use any drugs on the day of a scheduled therapy appointment. We will start each session by using this machine to measure your blood alcohol level. It is easy to use. I will hold it up to your mouth and you simply take a deep breath and blow through the tube for a few seconds until I tell you to stop.*

If deemed helpful, you may demonstrate how the Breathalyzer is used.

If the client has a positive BAL, ask about his or her drinking that day, and explain the relationship between amount of drinking and BAL. If BAL is above .05, further assess the client's drinking pattern and consider a detoxification program; if this does not seem indicated, you should reschedule the interview.

Brief Questionnaires

Each partner should be given a set of questionnaires to complete. It is most efficient to have the partners do this before the start of the assessment session, either by asking them to come 30 min early to the session and completing the forms in the waiting room or by sending the paperwork to the clients at home to complete beforehand.

Each partner should complete a general demographics survey including name, address, age, date of birth, employment status, occupation, children's names and ages, ethnicity, religion, marital status and years married or in a committed relationship.

Recommended instruments for the drinker include the following:

- *Personal Drinking Goal form.* This one-item questionnaire assesses the client's motivation for changing drinking patterns. The client rates his or her drinking goal on a 6-point scale ranging from "no change" to "lifelong abstinence" (adapted from Hall, Havassy, & Wasserman, 1991) on the form on the following page. If you need additional copies of this form, you may photocopy it from the book.

Personal Drinking Goal

Please read the goals listed below and choose the one that best represents your thoughts about drinking at this time by circling the number that corresponds to your goal.

1. I have decided not to change my pattern of drinking.

2. I have decided to cut down on my drinking and drink in a more controlled manner—to be in control of how often I drink and how much I drink. I would like to limit myself to no more than ___ drinks per _____ (days or weeks or months).

3. I have decided to stop drinking completely for a period of time, after which I will make a new decision about whether I will drink again. For me, the period of time I want to stop drinking is _____ (days, weeks, months, years).

4. I have decided to stop drinking regularly, but would like to have an occasional drink when I really have the urge.

5. I have decided to quit drinking once and for all, even though I realize I may slip up and drink once in a while.

6. I have decided to quit drinking once and for all, to be totally abstinent, and never drink alcohol ever again for the rest of my life.

7. None of this applies exactly to me. My own goal is:

- Marital functioning is assessed using three measures. First, the *Dyadic Adjustment Scale (DAS)* (Spanier, 1976; Busby, Christensen, Crane, & Larson, 1995) is a 2-item measure of relationship satisfaction. Scores are summed according to a template in the Spanier article and a cutoff of 106 is generally accepted as threshold below which the marriage is considered distressed. Second, the *Areas of Change Questionnaire (ACQ)* (Margolin, Talovic, & Weinstein, 1983) assesses desire for change in 34 areas of relationship functioning. Each partner indicates the degree of change they want in each area and then indicates the degree of change that they believe their partner wishes of them in the same 34 areas. Third, the *Modified Conflict Tactics Scale (MCTS)* is a 24-item self-report inventory of relationship aggression that occurred during the previous 12 months. Respondents answer each item for their own behavior and the behavior of their partner. Assessment of the non-drinker's coping may be done using *The Coping Questionnaire* (Copello, Templeton, & Velleman, 2006) to get a sense of how frequently the spouse uses strategies to alter antecedents and consequences of drinking.

- *The Beck Depression Inventory (BDI)* is a 21-item self-report instrument used to assess depression (Beck, Steer, & Garbin, 1988). BDI scores of 14–19 indicate mild depression, 20–28 indicate moderate depression, and 29–63 are suggestive of severe depression.

- *The Beck Anxiety Inventory (BAI)* is 21-item self-report instrument that measures symptoms of anxiety using a 4-point Likert-type scale (0–3) (Beck, Epstein, Brown, & Steer, 1988). BAI score thresholds are: 0–7 indicates "mild anxiety"; 16–25 "moderate"; and 26–63 "severe."

Initial Assessment: Presenting Problems, Role of Alcohol, Other Concerns, and How Drinking Has Affected the Partner and Relationship

Use the following worksheet to gather information on the client's problems (alcohol-related or otherwise) and how drinking has affected the relationship with his or her partner. Since you will likely use this form with more than one client, you may photocopy it from the book as needed.

1. *I'd like to get an idea of the sort of problems that have been troubling you. Can you tell me about them?*

   _____
   _____
   _____

2. *What have been the main difficulties that led you to seek help?*

   _____
   _____
   _____

3. *Are there any additional problems that concern you?*

   _____
   _____
   _____

4. Ask drinker: *How do you see the drinking as affecting your relationship?*

   _____
   _____
   _____

5. Ask partner: *How do you see the drinking problem(s)?*

   _____
   _____
   _____

6. Ask partner: *And how does this affect you?*

   _____
   _____
   _____

7. Ask partner: *Are there any additional problems that are concerning you?*

   _____
   _____
   _____

8. Ask partner: *How do you see the drinking as affecting your relationship?*

   _____
   _____
   _____

Assessment of Client's Drinking

Last use, length of problem, and quantity and frequency of alcohol use can be assessed through questions and instruments administered by the clinician. For instance, you can start off by asking the client the following:

- *When did you last have a drink of alcohol?* (month, day, time of day)
- *What and how much did you drink at that time?*
- *When and what did you drink the time before that?*
- *When did you have your first alcoholic drink when not under the supervision of your parents?*
- *When was the first time you became intoxicated?*
- *How many years has drinking been a problem for you?*

Then, you can move on to asking the client about the quantity and frequency of alcohol consumed over the past month or so. You may ask the following questions:

- *Over the past month or so, how many days per week have you had any alcohol to drink?*
- *What do you like to drink?*
- *Approximately how much do you usually drink?*
- *How long have you been drinking in this pattern?* (Get typical pattern of quantity/frequency in standard drinks—briefly)

Therapist Note

- *If the client has not had a drink in the past month or has been trying to cut down and therefore drinking at a lower level than usual, about the pattern of the last month and then ask again for the most recent pattern of problematic drinking. You may use the following questions:*

- *How many months/years did you drink in this general pattern?*

- *And what was your drinking pattern before that and how long did it last?*

This line of questioning will allow you to ascertain general patterns of drinking for recent and past history. Please note that questions regarding alcohol must be extremely detailed, in that you need to assess what type of alcoholic beverage the client drank, what proof the beverage was, how many ounces, the time the client began and stopped drinking for typical drinking occasions, and how much the client weighed at the time. This is the information you need in order to calculate number of standard drinks consumed, as well as approximate BAL. See Chapter 4 of this guide for a chart of standard drink conversion and a chart to calculate BAL. All alcohol consumption assessed is translated into standard drinks.

To get even more detailed information about a client's typical drinking pattern, use the Steady Pattern Grid in the Form-90 manual (Miller, 1996) to ascertain the pattern for a typical week. A copy of the Steady Pattern Grid is provided on the following page. If you need additional copies, you may photocopy the form from the book. For an assessment of a longer period of time, for instance over the 3 months prior to treatment entry, use the *Timeline Followback Interview (TLFB)* (Sobell & Sobell, 1996), which is a calendar method to obtain daily drinking data. In the Form-90 manual (Miller, 1996), there are instructions for using the pattern grid in conjunction with the Timeline Followback Interview.

Steady Pattern Grid From the Form-90

Please describe for me a usual or typical (heavy) week of drinking. In a typical week, let's start with weekdays—Monday through Friday—what did you normally drink in the morning, from the time you got up until lunchtime? (Do not include what was drank with lunch) (Record on Steady Pattern Chart)

Now how about weekday afternoons, including what you drank with lunch, up through the afternoon until (right *before*)*dinner time—what did you normally drink on weekday afternoons, Monday through Friday?* (Record on chart)

And how about weekday evenings? What did you normally drink with dinner, up through the rest of the evening, until the time you went to sleep? (Record on chart)

Repeat these same instructions for weekend days, and record on the chart.

Steady Pattern Chart

Day	Morning	Afternoon	Evening	Total standard drinks
MON				_____._____
TUE				_____._____
WED				_____._____
THU				_____._____
FRI				_____._____
SAT				_____._____
SUN				_____._____

The *Structured Clinical Interview for DSM-IV (SCID), Alcohol Use Disorders Module* (First, Spitzer, Gibbon, & Williams, 2002), yields lifetime and current alcohol abuse/dependence diagnoses. *DSM-IV* criteria for Alcohol Abuse and Alcohol Dependence are listed in Chapter 1 of this guide.

Negative consequences of use can be assessed through paper and pencil questionnaires such as the *Short Inventory of Problems (SIP)* or the *Drinker's Inventory of Consequences (DrInC),* both of which are public domain and can be accessed through this Web site: http://casaa.unm.edu/inst.htm. The SIP is a 15-item condensed version of the Drinker's Inventory of Consequences (DrInC), which has 50 items. Three items that are intended to assess lifetime problems with alcohol were taken from each of the DrInC subscales to comprise the SIP, including Physical, Intrapersonal, Social Responsibility, Interpersonal, and Impulse Control. The internal consistency and reliability for the SIP are high (alpha $=.81$, $r =.94$; Miller, Tonigan, & Longabaugh, 1995).

To assess for need for detoxification and level of care determination, take into account the last time client had an alcoholic drink (queried above) and ask: *"Are you currently feeling any of these withdrawal symptoms that I just listed? If so, which ones?"*

Determination of the need for detoxification is complex and based on multiple criteria. Some useful guidelines: (1) daily drinkers are more likely to need detoxification than episodic drinkers; (2) morning drinking (or drug use) or morning withdrawal symptoms suggest need for detoxification; (3) persons who drink on and off throughout the day are more likely to need detoxification than those who drink only in the evening; (4) high volume drinkers, who achieve a BAL above 200–250 mg, are likely to need detoxification; (5) persons with a history of withdrawal symptoms who are drinking regularly are likely to need detoxification; (6) persons with a history of withdrawal seizures or major withdrawal syndrome (disorientation, hallucinations) **must** get a medically supervised detoxification; (7) regular drinkers who have other medical problems (e.g. history of stroke, high blood pressure, liver disease) should have a medically supervised detoxification. If the clinician concludes that the client will need to be detoxified, this must be addressed at the conclusion of the interview. See Session 1 (Chapter 4) for an overview of abstinence plans, including consideration of level of care.

Assessment of Partner Drinking

This can be done using a quantity frequency index, for example, the National Institute on Alcohol Abuse and Alcoholism (NIAAA) Quantity Frequency Index (Armor, Polich, & Stambul, 1978). Partners can also be administered the SCID Alcohol and Drug section if partner use is a problem to obtain diagnoses. The Form-90 and Timeline Followback Interview can also be administered if the partner drinks heavily.

Assessment of Other Problems

Psychotic symptoms can be briefly assessed with the *SCID Psychotic Screen*. Should a screen be positive, the psychotic section from the SCID-I (First et al., 2002) can be administered. Depression and anxiety can be assessed using the BDI and BAI (see previous sections) or the SCID-I (First et al., 2002). Personality disorders can be assessed by the *SCID II* (First, Gibbon, Spitzer, & Williams, 1997). Cognitive impairment, if suspected, can be assessed briefly using the *Mini-Mental State Exam* (Folstein, Folstein, & McHugh, 1975). Health status and medications can be queried about in an open-ended way.

Use of illicit drugs can be assessed in brief using sections from the Brief or Comprehensive Drinker's Profile (Miller & Marlatt, 1984). Then, if the client has used drugs in the past years, the SCID drug section can be used to get more detailed information and diagnostic criteria for each class of drug used.

Assessment of Domestic Violence

Review the items endorsed by each partner on the MCTS (see previous related section) to see if either partner reported either initiating or experiencing severe domestic violence in the past year. If so, each partner should be seen privately for a few minutes to assess the circumstances around the violence, injuries sustained, the degree to which the violence occurs with or without intoxication, and fear of conjoint therapy. If the domestic violence is determined to be severe enough (threatening to use or use of a weapon, open-wound injuries, broken bones), couple therapy is not indicated, and each partner should be referred for individual therapy to address the violence as either a primary problem or in conjunction with treatment for the AUD. If the violence is less severe but still significant and is not secondary to drinking, and/or either partner is afraid that things said in marital therapy will spark more violence after the session, couple therapy is contraindicated.

Determining Level of Care

Level of care determination depends on several variables, including need for medically supervised detoxification (see previous information) based on severity of recent alcohol problem, medical history, history of withdrawal symptoms, psychiatric problems, past treatment experiences, support network, insurance considerations, and client preference (see Kadden & Skerker, 1999). In general, the treatment model in this manual is appropriate (1) as an aftercare program for clients who need a medically supervised detoxification initially to safely eliminate alcohol from their system, or (2) for clients who do not need or refuse a detoxification program but meet criteria for alcohol abuse or dependence *or* who are considered to be heavy drinkers because they drink more than 14 (for women) and 21 (for men) standard drinks per week (U.S. Department of Health and Human Services, National Institute of Health, 2003), or (3) for clients who do not need inpatient or intensive outpatient treatment. In all cases, clients need to have a spouse or significant other who is willing to participate in the treatment, should not have uncontrolled current psychiatric symptoms such as psychosis, mania, or suicidal ideation with intent or plan, and should not have recent history of non-alcohol-related domestic violence. Use the results of the assessment to determine the appropriate initial level of care for the client. Options for initial abstinence plans (including levels of care) are described in Session 1.

Giving Recommendations to the Couple

After the initial sessions and at the end of the assessment, be sure to give the couple some feedback. After the initial session, feedback could be phrased as follows:

You (the drinker) *clearly have concerns about your drinking, and I think these concerns are appropriate. I think you've made a good decision to look for some help. And, I'm confident that you'd benefit from the program. It appears that both of you have some legitimate concerns about the damaging effect of alcohol on your relationship, so in addition to helping* (drinker) *become abstinent and learn how to cope with difficult situations in your life, we will be able to focus on how you* (partner) *can support* (drinker) *in these efforts and also help you both repair and improve your communication and relationship satisfaction. What are your thoughts at this point about getting involved with our program?*

Need for Detoxification

If you determined that the drinker needs detoxification, give feedback about the need for detoxification, tailoring the specific content to the drinker's situation. A general suggested approach is as follows:

A little earlier I asked you a number of questions about your drinking pattern. From what you told me, it seems likely that you are physically dependent on alcohol and that you may need the help of a physician to stop drinking. This is called detoxification. It would be best for you to get some help to stop drinking before the treatment starts. There are two basic approaches to detoxification—inpatient or outpatient. In either case, you would receive medication for a few days to make it easier for you to get off the alcohol. You can do this either through a detoxification facility or as an outpatient.

You should recommend inpatient detoxification as the only option if the client has a history of withdrawal seizures, major withdrawal syndrome, or has significant medical problems.

You and the couple should then discuss options (see Session 1) and develop a specific plan. Chapter 1 discusses abstinence versus moderate drinking goals for this treatment approach and gives suggestions for how you can present the advantages of abstinence.

Summary

Assessment is considered a pivotal and integral part of CBT for alcohol-use problems. This chapter has provided an assessment plan that includes suggestions of areas to evaluate that are relevant to the treatment of alcohol misuse, as well as specific questions to ask in a clinical interview, and recommendations for self-report measures. Suggestions for providing feedback to the couple are provided here, and more detailed feedback using the assessment data is outlined in Session 1 of this manual. This assessment should allow you to get a detailed alcohol and drug history and a clear picture of current use and negative consequences of that use. The information obtained will allow you to determine level of care and services needed, as well as to develop an abstinence plan. In addition, this assessment covers several aspects of marital functioning useful to evaluate the need for and to conduct couple therapy. We find that clients often find the assessment phase of the treatment to be a valuable and therapeutic way to begin to examine their maladaptive drinking habits.

Chapter 4

Session 1: Introduction / Rationale / Self-Recording

(Corresponds to chapter 1 of the workbook)

Materials Needed

- Copy of couple's workbook
- Breathalyzer and 2 tubes
- Treatment Contract
- Feedback Sheets
- Supporting Change worksheet
- Partner and client self-recording cards
- Abstinence Plan worksheet
- High-Risk Situations worksheet
- Drinking Patterns Questionnaire (DPQ)

Outline

- Determine blood alcohol level (BAL) of both the client and his or her partner
- Make opening statements and build rapport (10 min)
- Provide treatment rationale (10 min)
- Discuss treatment requirements (5 min)
- Review data collected during intake assessment and complete Feedback Sheets (20 min)

- Talk to non-drinking partner about reasons for wanting to participate in treatment (10 min)

- Discuss partner's support for client's change (10 min)

- Introduce the concept of self-recording (10 min)

- Work with couple to draft an abstinence plan (optional) *and/or* address possible problem areas (optional) (5 min)

- Discuss ways to handle high-risk situations (5 min)

- Assign homework (5 min)

Therapist Note

■ *If the client is still drinking and needs an abstinence plan, leave more time in Session 1 for creating a plan.* ■

Before Session 1, review all data collected at the intake assessment. Extract specific information about the client's drinking patterns. Use the Short Inventory of Problems (SIP), Timeline Followback Interview, Form-90, and the intake interview. Extract information about partner coping behaviors around drinking and couple problems from the Coping Questionnaire, Dyadic Adjustment Scale (DAS), Areas of Change Questionnaire (ACQ), Modified Conflict Tactics Scale (MCTS), and the intake interview. (See Chapter 3 for more details.)

Also make sure that the couple has a copy of the workbook and remind both partners to bring the workbook to all sessions.

Blood Alcohol Level Determination

If the client's or partner's BAL is greater than .05, review treatment agreement and reschedule the session (see Chapter 2 for instructions to administer the Breathalyzer test).

Introductions: Opening Statements, Building Rapport (10 min)

Begin the session by providing an overview of the agenda and purpose of today's meeting. The focus of Session 1 is a discussion of the client's drinking patterns to enhance motivation, as well as the rationale for treatment and what the sessions will be like.

The rapport-building process should include both partners equally, asking both about their experiences with the assessment phase, any ways that they were influenced by the assessment, problems they are concerned about, and their goals for treatment.

Therapist Note

- *You should check possible urgent issues such as:*
- *Child safety*
- *Partner drinking or substance use*
- *Mood or anxiety disorders*

If the client reports an urgent issue, be sure to address the issue to the level that appears to be clinically appropriate. Check guidelines for dealing with the specific urgent issue provided in Chapter 1. If you have a supervisor or consultant, discuss with him or her how to deal with the particular issue.

Treatment Rationale (10 min)

When providing the treatment rationale, be sure to have an interactive discussion. Ask for both the client's and the partner's reactions and thoughts as you cover each point. The major points to discuss are: (1) reasons for entering treatment as a couple; (2) multiple foci of treatment—client's drinking, partner's coping, couple's relationship; (3) importance of individual responsibility for change and not blaming the other for problems; (4) goals of treatment.

You may use the following sample dialogue to present the rationale for treatment to the couple. The same dialogue also appears in the couple's workbook.

> *Together in this therapy, we are starting a journey. The most successful and ambitious journeys all start with a road map (a plan) and a destination (a goal). This therapy is part of the road map. The goals are sobriety and a happier relationship. The road map is this therapy.*

We will show you ways of quitting drinking and improving your life. We will work on identifying high-risk situations—those that may lead to drinking. Some of these situations will involve places, people, and things that you come across. Some of these situations will involve thoughts and emotions that are connected to your use. Some of these situations may come from your relationships. We will develop a plan and the skills to get through these tough situations. This journey will require dedication. In each session, we will provide a new skill or technique for dealing with high-risk situations.

The road will get bumpy at times. Sometimes things may be so rough that you will wonder if you've made a wrong turn. Many people who decide to quit drinking have a tough time in the beginning. Some people get discouraged by the tough times. Other people see these tough times as a chance to learn more about themselves. Whatever happens, we will look at these tough times as chances to learn more about what kinds of situations are risky and what it takes to get through them. When learning to ride a bicycle, most people will fall a few times. Most everyone gets back on the bicycle and eventually succeeds in learning to ride. You may go down the wrong path during our journey. If you do, recognizing this will be important so you can get back on the right road.

One very important part of this therapy is your commitment to working with me. Each week I will ask you to do things during the week. It is very important that you work hard at home. Work outside sessions is as important as work during sessions. Many individuals have succeeded with this program. The things taught in this program help people stop drinking and build better relationships.

Refer the couple to the description of the plan for treatment in the workbook. A copy for your use is provided on the following page.

The Plan

Over the course of this program you will:

1. Study your drinking habits. Figure out what leads to drinking and what keeps it going.

2. Change habits and things around you that lead to or encourage drinking.

3. Learn positive alternatives to drinking alcohol.

Your therapist will help you through these steps during the next 12 weeks. In the first three sessions, the focus will be on step one. As part of step one, you will look at what people, places, and things lead to drinking. You will also look at what happens because of drinking.

The following is a list of some important points about the treatment program you are about to begin.

- People with problems similar to yours have learned to stop drinking.

- Drinking is something you have learned to do. Habits can be changed. Right now, it does not matter how the drinking got started; it is important to figure out how to change.

- The goal is to be totally abstinent—to stop drinking altogether. Drinking should stop early on in the treatment. Sometimes people will have slips, but successful people learn from mistakes and get back with the program.

- Work in between sessions is as important as work during sessions. There will be things that you will be asked to do to learn and practice new skills. Practice is the only way to get this right. Often it is not possible to learn everything well during the session. If you do not complete the tasks required, your therapist reserves the right to reschedule your session in order to give you an opportunity to make up the work.

Continue the discussion of the treatment rationale:

> *We have asked you to come to treatment as a couple. This is because drinking affects other areas of your life, including your relationship and the family. In this program, we want both of you to have a road map to resolve the problems around alcohol. We will look at both your* (the client's) *drinking patterns, as well as your* (the partner's) *patterns that impact on drinking. That way we can help you both to deal more effectively with the drinking problem. If we worked with only one of you, the other one would have no idea what you were accomplishing in these sessions or what you were doing to not drink.*

> *Having you* (the partner) *here does not mean that I think you are to blame for your partner's drinking, only that you have been affected by it and may not know how best to cope with drinking situations or how to support your partner as he or she changes.* (Ask the couple if any of these observations ring true in their lives and how they feel about what you have just said.)

> *We have also found that in many couples where one person has a drinking problem there are also relationship problems. For one reason or another, couples no longer get the same satisfaction out of their relationship, and they may lose their ability to make decisions or solve problems. These problems may become roadblocks to reaching your goals, and therefore we must help you deal with these as well.* (Ask the couple if any of this is relevant to their current lifestyle. You may want to write down what they say for later sessions.)

Address the partner:

> *As you* (the partner) *may notice from the introduction to therapy, much of this treatment will focus on helping your partner to quit drinking. Especially at first, the treatment will concentrate on understanding and fixing the problem drinking. As therapy continues, we will place more attention on improving the way you get along with each other.*

> *We expect that your happiness with your relationship will increase as the drinking stops. In addition, we will use many techniques that have helped other couples become happier. All couples can benefit from this*

special attention, no matter how happy they are when they begin therapy.

We believe that you both will benefit from this experience. Imagine what life will be like without drinking and relationship problems!

We ask some things of you:

1. *Come to all the sessions with your partner. This treatment involves both of you.*
2. *Work on the assignments between sessions. What you see and experience during the week will help us succeed. I will ask you to observe and practice many things that will help both you and your partner.*
3. *Be patient! Both the drinking and any trouble in your relationship come from a long history of habits that have become well practiced over time. Both of you will need to work hard and long to change these habits. Big change will not happen overnight but will come with dedication to success.*
4. *Believe in yourself and your partner.*
5. *If you would like help with other problems of your own, let me know and I will guide you to the right kind of help.*

Address the drinker:

Together we will help you (the client) *to stop drinking (if you are not abstinent already) and help you to stay abstinent to the very best of your ability. This will be challenging for all of us and I expect some difficulties. This is where I will give you the help you need. I will help you in understanding your drinking and give you alternatives to control your drinking better. We will look at how your partner's behavior affects your drinking and equip him or her with another set of alternatives. We will also look at your relationship and help improve that. This means you will both get homework, and it is **essential** that you practice these new skills between therapy sessions. It is very hard to break old habits unless you do this.* (Ask the couple how they feel about this. Respond to issues such as denial, minimization, misconceptions about etiology, and lack of taking responsibility for behavior in a non-judgmental way.)

If you have any questions or are having a hard time please let me know, that's what I am here for.

Treatment Requirements (5 min)

Tell the couple that they should attend all sessions and arrive on time, call if they have to reschedule, refrain from drinking before sessions, and complete all homework assignments. Emphasize that the client—the individual with the drinking problem—will have total responsibility for carrying out his or her own treatment procedures and controlling drinking. This will be regardless of whatever the partner does or does not do. The partner will likewise take responsibility for carrying out the treatment procedures regardless of whatever the problem drinker does or does not do, including drinking. Stress to both client and partner that completing self-recording forms, questionnaires, and other homework assignments is critical for treatment success.

Have the couple read and sign a brief treatment contract at this time. A copy of the treatment contract is provided on the following page, as well as in the workbook. You may make photocopies as necessary.

Treatment Contract

1. I understand that this treatment will include 12 sessions over 3 months and I agree to participate for that length of time. If I want to withdraw from the program, I agree to discuss this decision with my therapist prior to taking this action.

2. I agree to attend all sessions and to be prompt. If it is absolutely necessary that I cancel a session, I will call in advance to reschedule. I also agree to call in advance if I will be late to a session.

3. (Drinker Only) I understand that this treatment is intended for people who want to abstain from alcohol. I understand that I must work on remaining clean and sober.

4. I agree that it is essential for me to come to the session alcohol-free. I understand that I will be asked to leave any session to which I come with a blood alcohol level of over .05. I will be required to arrange safe transportation home.

5. I understand that I will be given a breath test for alcohol use each session.

6. I understand that I will be expected to practice some of the skills I discuss in treatment. I agree to bring in the workbook with the completed homework each week to discuss with my therapist.

7. I will be expected to attend all scheduled weekly sessions as research has shown that this type of treatment is effective only if both partners attend scheduled appointments on a regular basis.

I have reviewed the above statements with my therapist and I agree to abide by them.

_____   _____
Client   Date

_____   _____
Partner   Date

_____   _____
Therapist   Date

Explain to the couple that you, as the therapist, also have several responsibilities. You will be at all scheduled sessions on time, will call if you have to reschedule, and will provide coverage when away.

Encourage the couple to call you during the week if any problems arise. Provide each partner with your contact information. Explain that you may bring up content from individual telephone conversations with either partner during therapy sessions. Having private or confidential conversations with one partner or the other often makes couple therapy less successful. At the same time, if there is an important issue that either partner believes must be kept confidential, listen carefully and make a judgment about how to handle the information disclosed.

Feedback From Intake Assessment (20 min)

Although the drinking part of the feedback process focuses primarily on the drinker, you should involve the partner in the process as well. Be aware that the partner may learn things about the client's drinking that he or she had not known previously. The partner should view this positively as an indication that his or her spouse/companion is being honest and taking the therapy seriously. Also explain to the couple that the feedback helps them both to understand where they are beginning and then allows them to see how the drinking progresses during treatment. During the feedback session, be sure to occasionally ask the partner if he or she has any questions.

Exercise—Feedback

Use the information garnered during the intake assessment to complete Feedback Sheets for the couple in session. We have included blank sheets for your use at the end of this chapter. You may photocopy them from the book and distribute to the couple. We have also included blank Feedback Sheets in the corresponding workbook. If you wish, you may provide the couple with data and have them fill out the sheets on their own.

Table 4.1 Alcohol Information

Beer

	Standard drinks			
Ounces	Light	Regular	European	Ice
12	.75	1	1.25	1.5
16	1	1.33	1.66	—

Wine 5 ounces = 1 standard drink

Amount	Ounces	Standard Drinks
750 ml	25.6	5
1.5 L	51	10

Hard Liquor
1.5 ounces of 80 proof liquor = 1 standard drink

Liquor			Equivalent number of standard drinks		
Amount	Street Name	Ounces	80 proof	100 proof	190 proof
	"Shot"	1.5	1	1.25	2.38
200 ml	"Half pint"	6.8	4.5	5.67	10.77
375 ml	"Pint"	12.75	8.5	10.63	20.19
750 m	"Fifth"	25.5	17	21.25	40.38
1.75 L	"Half Gallon"	59.5	40	49.58	94.21

Review these forms with the couple. Briefly review how to calculate standard drinks, using the information provided, and how to calculate BAL and percentile using the Alcohol Information table (Table 4.1), and the Blood Alcohol Level Estimation Charts (Table 4.2), and Percentile Table for Alcohol Use (Table 4.3).

Sample, completed Feedback Sheets are shown in Figures 4.1, 4.2, and 4.3.

Client Feedback

Summarize and provide feedback for the client using Feedback Sheet 1. This sheet addresses quantity of alcohol consumed and frequency of

Table 4.2 Blood Alcohol Level Estimation Charts

Men

Approximate Blood Alcohol Percentage

Drinks	\multicolumn{8}{c}{Body Weight in Pounds}	Sample Behavioral Effects
	100	120	140	160	180	200	220	240	
0	.00	.00	.00	.00	.00	.00	.00	.00	Only completely safe limit
1	.04	.03	.03	.02	.02	.02	.02	.02	Impairment begins
2	.08	.06	.05	.05	.04	.04	.03	.03	Driving skills significantly affected; Information processing altered
3	.11	.09	.08	.07	.06	.06	.05	.05	
4	.15	.12	.11	.09	.08	.08	.07	.06	
5	.19	.16	.13	.12	.11	.09	.09	.08	
6	.23	.19	.16	.14	.13	.11	.10	.09	Legally intoxicated; Criminal penalties; Reaction time slowed; Loss of balance; Impaired movement; Slurred speech
7	.26	.22	.19	.16	.15	.13	.12	.11	
8	.30	.25	.21	.19	.17	.15	.14	.13	
9	.34	.28	.24	.21	.19	.17	.15	.14	
10	.38	.31	.27	.23	.21	.19	.17	.16	

One drink is 1.5 oz. shot of hard liquor, 12 oz. of beer, or 5 oz. of table wine.

Women

Approximate Blood Alcohol Percentage

Drinks	\multicolumn{9}{c}{Body Weight in Pounds}	Sample Behavioral Effects
	90	100	120	140	160	180	200	220	240	
0	.00	.00	.00	.00	.00	.00	.00	.00	.00	Only completely safe limit
1	.05	.05	.04	.03	.03	.03	.02	.02	.02	Impairment begins
2	.10	.09	.08	.07	.06	.05	.05	.04	.04	Driving skills significantly affected; Information processing altered
3	.15	.14	.11	.10	.09	.08	.07	.06	.06	
4	.20	.18	.15	.13	.11	.10	.09	.08	.08	
5	.25	.23	.19	.16	.14	.13	.11	.10	.09	
6	.30	.27	.23	.19	.17	.15	.14	.12	.11	Legally intoxicated; Criminal penalties; Reaction time slowed; Loss of balance; Impaired movement; Slurred speech
7	.35	.32	.27	.23	.20	.18	.16	.14	.13	
8	.40	.36	.30	.26	.23	.20	.18	.17	.15	
9	.45	.41	.34	.29	.26	.23	.20	.19	.17	
10	.51	.45	.38	.32	.28	.25	.23	.21	.19	

One drink is 1.5 oz. shot of hard liquor, 12 oz. of beer or 5 oz. of table wine.

Subtract .015 for each hour that you take to consume the number of drinks listed in the table. For example, if you are a 160 pound woman and have two drinks in two hours, your BAC would be .06 - (2 x .015) = .03

NOTE: Blood Alcohol Level (BAL) charts do not take into consideration a wide range of additional variables that contribute to the determination of BAL's achieved and the behavioral effects experienced at a given BAL. These additional variables include: age, water-to-body-mass ratio, ethanol metabolism, tolerance level, drugs or medications taken, amount and type of food in the stomach during consumption, speed of consumption, and general physical condition. Thus, BAL charts only provide extremely rough estimates and should never be used alone to determine any individual's safe level of drinking.

Adapted from BAC Charts produced by the National Clearinghouse for Alcohol and Drug Information.

drinking, percentile of alcohol consumption, estimated peak BAL in a typical week, estimated average blood alcohol concentration (BAC) in a typical week, and severity of the AUD as determined by the SIP and SCID measures administered during intake assessment. Also describe to

Table 4.3 Percentile Table for Alcohol Use

Drinks per week	Total	Men	Women
0	35	29	41
1	58	46	68
2	66	54	77
3	68	57	78
4	71	61	82
5	77	67	86
6	78	68	87
7	80	70	89
8	81	71	89
9	82	73	90
10	83	75	91
11	84	75	91
12	85	77	92
13	86	77	93
14	87	79	94
15	87	80	94
16	88	81	94
17	89	82	95
18	90	84	96
19	91	85	96
20	91	86	96
21	92	88	96
22	92	88	97
23–24	93	88	97
25	93	89	98
26–27	94	89	98
28	94	90	98
29	95	91	98
30–33	95	92	98
34–35	95	93	98
36	96	93	98
37–39	96	94	98
40	96	94	99
41–46	97	95	99
47–48	97	96	99
49–50	98	97	99
51–62	98	97	99
63–64	99	97	>99.5
65–84	99	98	>99.6
85–101	99	99	>99.9
102–159	>99.5	99	>99.9
160+	>99.8	>99.5	>99.9

Source: 1990 National Alcohol Survey, Alcohol Research Group, Berkeley. Courtesy of Dr. Robin Room.

the client three to six negative consequences he or she reported during pre-treatment assessment. This review will begin to set the stage for functional analysis, self-awareness, and change.

You may use the following sample dialogue:

> *Based on the information we obtained at the assessment session, I calculated the number of "standard drinks" you consumed in a typical week, during the 3 months before you came here. You have been drinking an average of _____ standard drinks per week and an average of _____ standard drinks per drinking day. This places you in the _____ percentile of men/women in America, in terms of drinking. In other words, you have been drinking more than approximately _____ percent of the population of men/women in America, and more than _____ percent of the population of adults in America. (Refer to Table 4.3)*
>
> *I also estimated your peak and typical blood alcohol concentration (BAC) in the last 3 months. Your BAC is based on how many standard drinks you consume, the length of time over which you drink that many standard drinks, whether you are a male or female, and how much you weigh. So, for instance, if we use these tables for the amount of alcohol you typically drink per drinking occasion, at your weight and over the amount of time it typically takes you to consume this amount of alcohol, your peak (highest) BAC for the past 3 months or so was _____. Your typical BAC for the past 3 months or so has been _____. This is a measure of how intoxicated you typically become. There is a table in your workbook outlining the impairment people suffer based on different BACs.*

Refer the client to Table 4.4 on page 69, which is also found in the workbook:

> *You have told us about several negative consequences you experience from drinking* (discuss the negative consequences the client identified during the pre-treatment assessment phase).

Table 4.4 Common Effects of Different Levels of Intoxication

.02–.06%	This is the "normal" social drinking range. Driving, even at these levels, is unsafe.
.08%	Memory, judgment, and perception are impaired. Legally intoxicated in most states.
.1%	Reaction time and coordination of movement are affected. Legally intoxicated in all states.
.15%	Vomiting may occur in normal drinkers; balance is often impaired.
.2%	Memory "blackout" may occur, causing loss of recall for events occurring while intoxicated.
.3%	Unconsciousness in a normal person, though some remain conscious at levels in excess of .6% if tolerance is very high.
.4–.5%	Fatal dose for a normal person, though some survive higher levels if tolerance is very high.

For the Drinker:

1. Based on the information I obtained during the assessment, I calculated the number of "standard drinks" you consumed in a typical week during the last 3 months before you came in :

    Total number of standard drinks per week   __143__

    Average number of standard drinks per drinking day   __20.4__

2. When we look at everyone who drinks in the United States, you have been drinking more than approximately __99__ percent of the population in the country.

3. I also estimated your highest and average blood alcohol level (BAL) in the past 3 months. Your BAL is based on how many standard drinks you consume, the length of time over which you drink that much, whether you are a man or a woman, and how much you weigh. So,

    Your estimated peak BAL in the past 3 months was   __.50__

    Your estimated typical BAL in an average week was   __.27__

4. You have experienced many negative consequences from drinking. Here are some of the most important:

    __Blackouts__   __Physical violence__

    __Hospitalization__   __Depression__

    __Making people afraid__   __Missing work__

Figure 4.1
Example of Completed Feedback Sheet 1

Partner Feedback

Use Feedback Sheet 2 to summarize for the couple the ways in which the non-drinking partner has attempted to cope with the client's alcohol use. Be sure to note the coping behaviors the partner endorsed most frequently on The Coping Questionnaire completed during pre-treatment assessment. Select both positive and maladaptive types of coping.

Couple Feedback

Use Feedback Sheet 3 to summarize for the couple any relationship issues they brought up during the pre-treatment assessment, as well as scores and problems from the DAS and ACQ questionnaires that the drinker completed. Ask the client what areas he or she has most concern

---

For the Partner:

5. Based on the information you provided during the assessment, you have made a number of attempts to support your partner in not drinking:

   Talking with her about her desire to drink   *Complimenting her*

   Doing things together   *Making sure there is no alcohol in the house*

   Eating meals together at regular times   *Showing her affection*

6. You've also reacted to your partner's drinking in a number of ways that probably have been less helpful:

   Making her comfortable when she drank   *Doing her chores for her*

   Arguing with her to try to make her stop drinking   *Pretending to others that all is well*

   Pleading with her not to drink   *Asking her employer to step in*

Figure 4.2

Example of Completed Feedback Sheet 2

For the Couple:

1. The two of you both see certain problems or concerns about your relationship:

   Arguments   Time together vs. time for ourselves

   Violence   Financial responsibility

   Extramarital affairs

2. There are some problems or concerns, however, that one of you has emphasized more than the other:

   Client's concerns: **Partner's concerns:**

   More time with my friends and family   I want more attention

   Want my partner to be more responsible   I want to be appreciated more

   My partner should help me with the   I want more sex and physical intimacy
   housework

Figure 4.3
Example of Completed Feedback Sheet 3

about in the relationship. Describe for the couple what seem to be the three to six most important relationship problems they have described.

Ask the client and partner to comment on the feedback provided. Listen attentively, convey understanding verbally and nonverbally, and indicate that clients with similar drinking problems have successfully utilized this treatment (establish positive expectancy).

Therapist Note

■ *Tell the client that it's always a good idea to see his or her physician for a checkup and to get a blood test to check on liver function, since alcohol is a toxin and heavy drinking can affect the liver and other vital organs. A list of specific hepatic function tests is included in the workbook. Ask the client to bring lab results in to show you. See Allen and Litten (2001) for information on how to interpret lab tests.*

Tell the client to specifically request the following tests:

Gamma glutamic transpeptidase (GGTP)

Aspartate aminotransferase (AAT)

Alanine aminotransferase (ALAT)

Mean corpuscular volume (MCV)

Bilirubin

Uric acid ■

Increasing Partner Motivation for Treatment (10 min)

Because partners of drinkers are sometimes ambivalent about treatment, it is important to touch base with the partner's feelings about participating in this program. Ask him or her to talk a little bit about the reasons for wanting to go to treatment, or any reasons for not wanting to go. You may use the following sample dialogue:

Even though we have asked you to attend treatment sessions together and I have described reasons why couple therapy is valuable, I know that partners sometimes have some ambivalence about being involved in the treatment. Therefore, I want to touch base about how you (the partner) feel about participating in treatment sessions.

Address the partner:

Tell me a bit about the reasons you wanted to participate in this treatment. Did you have any reasons you didn't want to come?

Ask the client for reactions to what his or her partner has said. If necessary, you may suggest other reasons the partner may want to participate in treatment.

Some partners may feel quite angry and resentful toward the drinker because of problems related to the drinking and may feel reluctant to participate in treatment. Explain to the partner that the treatment is structured as couple treatment partly to allow him or her to express these feelings. The partner's expression of these negative feelings can help motivate the drinker to become abstinent.

Help the partner weigh the positive and negative consequences of participating or not participating in treatment. You may express your clinical opinion to add weight to the positive side of participating.

Partner Support for Drinker's Change (10 min)

Use the following dialogue to discuss the importance of partner support.

Changing a habit like heavy drinking is difficult. You can help! Small things can help the other person keep trying. One thing you can do is to say pleasant things that show you notice your partner's efforts. Compliments have powerful effects on other people. Focus them on the positives (say "You look nice today"); avoid reminding your partner of negatives (don't say "You don't look so puffy since you stopped drinking"). Talk together about pleasant things you can say to show your appreciation. Your words of encouragement can keep your partner going.

Often people say things to others and assume they are saying something nice. People make many mistakes when they assume something about another person. Other people do not always understand what we say. Everyone has an example of someone else taking a comment the wrong way. You will avoid trouble by asking your partner what he or she finds helpful. Develop a list of things that he or she would like to hear. Work out an agreement on three or four comments you will say to your partner for encouragement. Tell your partner that these are things that you will say as recognition for trying hard.

Do things to show your appreciation. Your actions will keep your partner going as well. Think of some small ways to show your appreciation. Leaving your partner a note, calling during the day, emailing, and bringing home something your partner likes can all help. Talk with your partner to find out what he or she would like. Don't assume that you know. Make a list of your ideas and try them out.

Some days you may find it hard to be supportive. You may start thinking of the problems your partner's drinking has caused. You may feel angry and resentful at times. These feelings are normal, but if you dwell on them, they will only get worse. Remind yourself that your partner wants to change and is trying to change. If you help, you'll both get what you want in the end!

Exercise—Support for Change

Ask the couple to think about ways that the non-drinking partner might provide support or encouragement to the client every week. These should be fairly small actions that are easy to implement. For example, a hug at the end of the day if the client wasn't drinking, a verbal expression of appreciation for something the client did whether or not it was related to drinking ("You're doing great," "I'm proud of you," "I had fun with you today"), doing a chore, or helping around the house. The partner should select three things to do during the week to communicate support to the client for being in treatment and starting to change. Have the couple write these down on the Supporting Change worksheet in the workbook. A sample completed worksheet is shown in Figure 4.4.

Supporting Change

List 3 to 6 actions that you could do to support your partner in changing.

1. Give her a hug when she gets home
2. Don't bring up things from the past
3. Tell her I love her
4. Tell her I'm proud of her for not drinking today
5. Remove all alcohol from the house
6. Don't drink in front of her when we go out to eat

Figure 4.4
Example of Completed Supporting Change Worksheet

Self-Recording (10 min)

Self-monitoring is when the drinker writes down what he or she does on a daily basis. Explain to the couple that recording drinking and urges to drink will help everyone get a better idea of what is going on. Monitoring will help the client identify patterns in his or her life and figure out different chains of behaviors that lead to drinking. You may use the following sample dialogue to further explain the importance of self-monitoring:

An important part of treatment is to work with facts, with accurate information. In our case, we want to learn about what happens during your day. The best way to collect facts is to write them down as they happen. Trying to recall things later is difficult. Everyone makes mistakes when they try to figure out what happened some time back, whether it was a few days ago or yesterday.

With self-monitoring, drinkers are surprised with how much they are drinking and that their drinking falls into patterns that happen over and over. It also helps us to realize how often you are getting urges or desires to drink and what leads to these urges. We will learn how you are able to beat back some urges already. Some urges will be tougher than others. We will learn more about which ones are easier than others. The monitoring will help us see your progress as we go through this program.

We will also look at how your satisfaction with your relationship changes from day to day. Every relationship has good and bad days. We will see a general improvement in your relationship as this program continues.

On the cards provided in your workbook, you should write down your urges to drink, any drinks or drugs you may have had, and how satisfied you are with your relationship.

You will need to do this everyday. I will help you figure out a way to remember to record every day. One suggestion is to keep the cards in a place with other things that you always have with you. When you have a drink or have an urge, write it down as soon as possible. Don't rely on your memory later.

An appendix of self-recording cards is included in the corresponding workbook. Since clients will need to carry their self-recording cards with them at all times, they have been placed on perforated sheets enabling the client to tear them out of the workbook.

The client will be asked to keep:

- A daily record of drinking behavior;
- A daily record of urges or thoughts of drinking (both quantity and strength);
- A daily relationship satisfaction rating; and
- If female, whether she is menstruating.

The partner will use one self-monitoring card per week to record the following:

- Whether or not he or she thinks the client had anything to drink that day (abstinent, light (1–2 drinks), moderate (3–4 drinks), or heavy (5 or more drinks));
- An overall rating of the client's drinking urges, and
- A daily relationship satisfaction rating.

The partner should not ask the client how much he or she drank, or try to check up on him or her. The partner should simply record his or her best estimate based on personal observations of the client's behavior.

Self-recording responses should be taught through modeling and role-playing with feedback in order to ensure that the procedures are clearly understood.

Tell the client to carry the self-recording cards at all times, one per day. If the client drinks, he or she should record before each drink (i.e., record each drink separately). Instruct the client to include details about what type of drink (e.g., "Bud Light" or "white wine"), how much (ounces), and the situation in which the drinking occurred. Also, the client should record each thought or urge immediately and its intensity on a 1–7 scale (7 = most intense). Tell the client that urges may occur for months after cessation of drinking. This is normal and to be expected.

Provide the client with the following instructions for completing the card. These same instructions can be found in the workbook as well.

> *Make sure to write in the date that you are filling in the card. You should fill in a card for every day of the week. We will use this information to look at patterns that happen across the week.*
>
> *Under "Urges," write down at what time the urge happened and how intense it was. For intensity, put down a number between 1 and 7 to describe how strong the urge was. Number 1 would mean that the urge was very weak. Number 7 would mean that the urge was one of the strongest ones that you have ever felt. If the urge was somewhere in the middle, then give it a number in between. Write down what triggered the urge.*
>
> *If you drink, under the "Drinks" section put in some information about what you drank, how much you drank, and the amount of alcohol in the drink. In the column labeled "Time," write down when you started drinking. Record the type of drink you had in the column labeled "Type of Drink." In the column labeled "Amount," write down how many drinks you had and the size of each drink. One way to do this is to know the size of the glass and how much liquid it holds. We often tell people to measure their drinks so they can understand how much they are drinking. In the column labeled "% Alcohol," write down the alcohol content of the drink you are having. Drinks other than beer will have this on the bottle or can.*
>
> *In the "Trigger" section, record the event that led to the drinking.*
>
> *Where it says "Relationship Satisfaction" on the card, write down how satisfied you are with your relationship each day. Also use a number between 1 and 7 to rate your satisfaction. If you are not satisfied at all, circle 1. If you are extremely satisfied, circle 7. If you are in between, pick a number that represents how satisfied you are.*

(For female clients only:) *Lastly, indicate whether you are menstruating by circling "yes" or "no" on the card.*

Provide the partner with the following instructions for completing the card. These same instructions can be found in the workbook as well.

> *Make sure to write in the date of when you are filling in the card.*
>
> *Circle the amount of drinking you think your partner did during the day. You may not always be sure; make your best guess. There are four different levels of drinking:*
>
> *NO—Circle NO if your partner did not drink that day.*
>
> *L—Circle L if your partner drank 1 or 2 drinks that day.*
>
> *M—Circle M if your partner drank 3 or 4 drinks that day.*
>
> *H—Circle H if your partner drank 5 or more drinks that day.*
>
> *If your partner used drugs that day, circle Y in the "Drug Use" section. If your partner does not use any drugs or did not use drugs on that day, circle N.*
>
> *In the section labeled "Urge Intensity," circle a number that represents the intensity of urges to drink experienced by your partner during the day. Use a number between 0 and 7 to indicate the size of the urges. If your partner suffers no urges, circle 0. If your partner's urges are extremely intense, circle 7. If the urges are not as great, circle a number somewhere in the middle. We would like to know the overall intensity of urges experienced during the day.*
>
> *Also be sure to record your level of relationship satisfaction on the card by circling a number between 1 and 7. If you are not satisfied at all, circle 1. If you are extremely satisfied, circle 7. If you are in between, pick a number that represents how satisfied you are.*
>
> *Your contribution is important to this treatment. We will use the information to help your partner stop drinking. In addition, we will use the information to help improve your relationship. Remember to write down your observations every day!*

Examples of completed self-recording cards for both the client and the partner are shown in Figures 4.5 and 4.6.

Daily monitoring

Date 10/8/08

Urges

Time	How strong? (1–7)	Trigger
8:00 a.m.	4	Traffic during commute
5:30 p.m.	7	Irritated when I came home

Drinks

Time	Type of drink	Amount (in ounces)	% Alcohol	Trigger
6:00 p.m.	Wine	1 bottle 25 oz.	12%	Fight with John

Relationship Satisfaction   1   2   ③   4   5   6   7

very low   greatest ever

For woman only   Do you have your menstrual period today?   Yes   (No)   N/A

Figure 4.5

Example of Completed Client Self-Recording Card

Partner monitoring

Day	Date	Drinking	Drug use	Urge intensity	Relationship satisfaction
Monday	10/6/08	NO L M (H)	Y (N)	0 1 2 3 4 5 (6) 7	1 2 (3) 4 5 6 7
Tuesday	10/7/08	NO L (M) H	Y (N)	0 1 2 3 (4) 5 6 7	1 2 3 4 (5) 6 7
Wednesday	10/8/08	NO L M (H)	Y (N)	0 1 2 3 4 (5) 6 7	1 2 (3) 4 5 6 7
Thursday	10/9/08	NO (L) M H	Y (N)	0 1 (2) 3 4 5 6 7	1 2 3 4 5 (6) 7
Friday	10/10/08	NO L M (H)	Y (N)	0 1 2 3 4 5 6 (7)	(1) 2 3 4 5 6 7
Saturday	10/11/08	NO L M (H)	Y (N)	0 1 2 3 4 5 6 (7)	(1) 2 3 4 5 6 7
Sunday	10/12/08	NO L M (H)	Y (N)	0 1 2 3 (4) 5 6 7	1 (2) 3 4 5 6 7

Figure 4.6

Example of Completed Partner Recording Card

Exercise—Self-Recording

Model self-recording responses, then ask the client for a typical drinking situation and have him or her role-play self-recording. Role-play problem situations and alternative responses, such as the following:

- "What if someone asks me what I'm doing?"—Sample alternatives: Tell them straight; or say, "I am on a diet," etc.

- "This is an abstinence program. What if I drink?"—Tell the client that you do not encourage drinking and generally will not hold sessions when the client's BAL is greater than .05; however, you want the client to be honest when recording so that you can teach skills for abstaining in situations that are difficult.

Stress the fact that self-recording has been found to increase self-awareness and its important role in self-control. Self-recording is also part of treatment, that is, becoming aware of chains of triggers, behaviors, and consequences that were hidden before.

Abstinence Plan for Client Still Drinking and/or Possible Problem Areas (5 min)

Problem issues should be addressed *only* if clients raise them.

Present the following rationale to the client:

The first step in treatment is helping you to actually stop drinking. Then we will move on, throughout the treatment, to teaching you skills to stay sober, prevent relapse, cope better with problems, etc. Let's talk about the first step.

There are several options for stopping your use of alcohol. Let me review the options and then we can discuss the ones that appeal to you most.

Discuss the following options for stopping drinking with your client: (1) inpatient detoxification, (2) outpatient detoxification, (3) going "cold turkey," and (4) stopping on your own, with the help of the therapist.

Inpatient Detoxification

One option is inpatient detoxification. There are hospitals in the area that do this. This means that you would go to a hospital detox or rehab unit and stay there between 3 and 7 days. They would probably give you some medicine during this time to relieve withdrawal symptoms. The advantage of an inpatient detox is that you are medically supervised, will avoid most withdrawal symptoms since you'll be medicated, and it's a quick way to get the alcohol out of your system and "start fresh" in this program as your aftercare. The disadvantage to inpatient detox is that some people don't want to stay in a hospital for a few days, and some people don't have insurance to cover this. I strongly recommend inpatient detox for patients who are very heavy drinkers and those who are unable to stop drinking on their own. Also, it is essential for anyone who is at risk for medical complications during withdrawal (personal or family history of seizures, stroke, high blood pressure, cardiac problems, etc.).

Outpatient Detoxification

Another option is outpatient detoxification. This is where you would go see a physician—either your family doctor or a doctor who specializes in outpatient detoxification—on an outpatient basis. Each doctor may do an outpatient detox in his or her own way; typically, doctors who do outpatient detox will prescribe enough medication to last a couple of days and then have you come back for an evaluation and determine whether medication is needed for a few more days, depending on the severity of your withdrawal symptoms. The advantage to an outpatient detoxification is that, similar to inpatient detoxification, you get it over with quickly. Within a week, you will have stopped using alcohol and passed through the initial more severe withdrawal symptoms with medication to help ease them. Another advantage is that you are under a physician's care, in case there are medical complications. A disadvantage to outpatient detox is that you must not drink alcohol while you are taking the medication the doctor prescribes, and some patients end up using both, which is extremely dangerous.

Going "Cold Turkey"

A third option is for you to stop on your own, or go "cold turkey." I recommend this option only for people who drink episodically rather than daily, who have no history of withdrawal symptoms when they stopped in the past, who are not at risk medically (high blood pressure, history of stroke, etc.), and who are not extremely heavy drinkers. For heavy, regular drinkers, going cold turkey with no medical supervision can result in uncomfortable withdrawal symptoms at best, and, at worst, serious medical complications such as seizures. Also, withdrawal symptoms are often triggers for relapse.

Stopping on Your Own With the Help of a Therapist

A fourth option for certain individuals is to wind down yourself, with my help. We would work together and agree on a schedule for you to gradually stop your use of alcohol over the next few weeks. We would set a quit date, and then work toward that date. Gradually decreasing your alcohol consumption will reduce, but probably not eliminate, withdrawal symptoms. So, for instance, we will take out a calendar and plan for how much you can drink each week, and we'll make sure that it is always either a plateau or a reduction from one day to the next—otherwise you'll experience withdrawal if you cut back a lot one day and then use more the next, and you'll have to go through withdrawal all over again. The advantage to this method is that you don't have to go somewhere inpatient or see a doctor. It is gradual, so you will be able to avoid major withdrawal symptoms, but you must be prepared to experience some withdrawal problems since you won't be medicated. You'd be at less risk for the medical dangers of going cold turkey if you're a daily heavy user. A disadvantage of this approach is that since it is gradual, it does take some time, and some people feel they would rather just get over with it quickly than spread out the reduction and associated withdrawal symptoms over a few weeks. Another disadvantage is that this approach takes a lot of planning and willpower on your part, especially in the beginning. I will help you, but you have to expect some challenges.

Engage both partners in the decision about how to achieve abstinence. See Figure 4.7. for a sample abstinence plan.

Abstinence Plan

I will check myself into a detox center this weekend and do what they tell me to do. I will not stop "cold turkey" because that will put me at risk for major withdrawal symptoms if I am not in a hospital at the time.

Figure 4.7
Example of Completed Abstinence Plan

Possible Problem Areas

Some clients or partners believe that all they need is "willpower" in order to change. Respond to this by telling the client that he or she needs to develop ways to carry out his or her will.

Some clients may ask, "What if I start drinking or binge?" In all probability, this question will arise at some point during treatment. A possible response may be:

> *Breaking a problem drinking habit is a difficult undertaking that necessitates a total commitment to change on the part of the client. This treatment program is designed to help you remain abstinent, teaching you the skills of self-control. If you feel that you are losing control or are about to drink, the rule of thumb is "to leave fast" and then use your self-recording as a way to analyze your thoughts/urges. If you drink, remember, "One drink does not mean drunk." We have treated people who have had one drink and stopped, have binged 3 days and then been abstinent, even people who have had to be hospitalized but who subsequently have remained sober. The majority of clients remain abstinent. If you are committed to the treatment, you will succeed.*

The idea is to communicate the fact that the treatment goal is abstinence but that "slips" do not equal treatment failure. It has been documented that one factor affecting relapse rate is client expectancy. If the client feels that having one drink means "loss of control," he or she will probably keep drinking. Convey to the client that "loss of control" is partly "in the head." Remind the client that he or she can always call you (before drinking) if other alternatives have been exhausted and drinking seems inevitable. It is important for you to convey a non-judgmental attitude and openness when discussing drinking. If the client can discuss drinking freely, then appropriate intervention measures can be implemented.

Clients may also ask, "Should I go to AA/NA meetings?" A possible response may be:

> *If you are already going to Twelve Step meetings, you can continue to go if you find it helpful. If you are interested in a support group, some individuals find Alcoholics Anonymous helpful. There are also support groups based on the same principles of cognitive-behavioral therapy that we are using in this program. One such group is called SMART Recovery®, and I can help you find meetings if you are interested.*

Anticipating High-Risk Situations This Week (5 min)

You may use the following sample dialogue to discuss high-risk situations with the couple:

> *At the end of each session, we will spend a bit of time discussing any problem situations that you think might come up around drinking this week. As you progress through therapy, you will get better and better at anticipating and handling these. A "high-risk situation" is a situation in which you would find it very difficult not to drink. Today, I'd like us to spend a few minutes together thinking about the upcoming week. Are there any situations that you might encounter this week that would tempt you to drink?*

Exercise—High-Risk Situations

Work with the client to identify at least one high-risk situation coming up in the next week. Instruct the client to write down ideas about how to handle this situation on the High-Risk Situations worksheet in the workbook. Also ask the client to write down on the back of a self-recording card how he or she actually handled the anticipated situation and to write down any other situations that were not anticipated. An example of a completed High-Risk Situations worksheet is given in Figure 4.8.

Therapist Note

■ *Be sure to include the partner in this discussion. He or she may help anticipate a high-risk situation, may have a helpful perspective about the situation or people involved, or may have ideas about what might help. The ultimate plan, however, must be one with which the client feels comfortable.* ■

High-Risk Situations

What high-risk situations do you think you may experience this week?

Situation 1: Friday—end of the work week—will want a reward for working hard

How can you handle this situation?

- Tell myself that being sober is a gift
- Go to the gym instead of the bar
- Get my girlfriend to take a bubble bath with me

Situation 2: Have to get child support payment to my ex-wife

How can you handle this situation?

- Put the check in her mailbox when she's not home
- Get a pizza after I drop off the check and bring it home
- Ask my brother to drop off the check for me

Figure 4.8
Example of Completed High-Risk Situations Worksheet

Homework (5 min)

- Instruct the client to record alcohol use, urges (intensity, frequency), and relationship satisfaction on a daily basis using the client self-recording cards.

- Ask the client to record the occurrence of high-risk situations, and how he or she handled those that were discussed in session.

- Instruct the partner to record the client's alcohol use and urges (intensity), and his or her own level of relationship satisfaction using the partner recording cards.

- Have the partner implement the plan to support the drinker as outlined in the Supporting Change worksheet.

- Have each partner complete the Drinking Patterns Questionnaire (DPQ) (regarding the drinker's patterns, not the partner's) and bring it to the next session. The DPQ can be found at the end of the book. You may photocopy and distribute as necessary.

- Instruct the couple to read Chapter 1 of the workbook.

- Have the client make an appointment with his or her general practitioner to have a physical checkup and to get blood tests to check liver function (see pages 71 & 72 for a list of specific tests).

Feedback Sheet 1

For the Drinker:

1. Based on the information I obtained during the assessment, I calculated the number of "standard drinks" you consumed in a typical week during the last 3 months before you came in :

    Total number of standard drinks per *week* _____

    Average number of standard drinks per *drinking day* _____

2. When we look at everyone who drinks in the United States, you have been drinking more than approximately _____ percent of the population in the country.

3. I also estimated your highest and average blood alcohol level (BAL) in the past 3 months. Your BAL is based on how many standard drinks you consume, the length of time over which you drink that much, whether you are a man or a woman, and how much you weigh. So,

    Your estimated *peak BAL* in the past 3 months was _____

    Your estimated *typical BAL* in an average week was _____

4. You have experienced many negative consequences from drinking. Here are some of the most important:

    _____

    _____

    _____

Feedback Sheet 2

For the Partner:

5. Based on the information you provided during the assessment, you have made a number of attempts to support your partner in not drinking:

_____

_____

_____

6. You've also reacted to your partner's drinking in a number of ways that probably have been less helpful:

_____

_____

_____

Feedback Sheet 3

For the Couple:

1. The two of you both see certain problems or concerns about your relationship:

_____

_____

_____

2. There are some problems or concerns however, that one of you has emphasized more than the other:

Client's concerns: **Partner's concerns:**

_____ _____

_____ _____

_____ _____

Chapter 5

Session 2: Functional Analysis / Noticing Positive Behavior

(Corresponds to chapter 2 of the workbook)

Materials Needed

- Copy of couple's workbook
- Breathalyzer and 2 tubes
- Client and partner self-recording cards
- Alcohol Use and Urges Graph
- Relationship Satisfaction Graph
- List of Triggers worksheet
- Behavior Chain worksheet
- Notice Something Nice worksheet
- High-Risk Situations worksheet

Outline

- Determine blood alcohol level (BAL) of both the client and his or her partner
- Provide overview of session (5 min)
- Review self-recording and homework (5 min)
- Check in (10 min)
- Perform a functional analysis with the client to determine triggers for drinking (35 min)

- Introduce the concept of "notice something nice" (20 min)
- Identify potential upcoming high-risk situations and plan for how to cope with them (10 min)
- Assign homework (5 min)

Blood Alcohol Level Determination

If the client's or partner's BAL is greater than .05, reschedule the session. If the client is still drinking, remind client of the abstinence plan and revise if necessary.

Overview of Session and Set Agenda (5 min)

Explain to the couple what will be covered in this session. Ask them if there is anything pressing they would like to discuss today in addition to the planned material.

Review Self-Recording and Homework (5 min)

At the beginning of this and subsequent sessions, review and collect completed self-recording cards from the client and partner. If homework is not done, ask what made it difficult. Completion of homework should be discussed and clarified, and a firm commitment for the future should be stressed in a non-judgmental way. You should then reconstruct the urge, drinking, and relationship satisfaction data for the week (See section "Graphing Progress"). This includes daily drinking and urges and daily relationship ratings. Reinforce self-recording behavior, screen for questions or problems, and help the client develop solutions for difficulties related to self-recording. The following conversation between client (C) and therapist (T) provides an example of how to help the client accurately record urges to drink.

C: I thought about drinking the whole morning. Is that one urge thought or more than one?

T: You had the urge continually?

C: Not every minute.

T: Well, each time you think about having a specific type of drink or a drink in a particular situation that counts as a separate urge. Can you give me some specific situations you thought about?

At this point in the session, review the client's recording of high-risk situations and how he or she handled them.

Review the partner's recording of the client's drinking and urges. Also review the partner's level of relationship satisfaction as indicated on the recording card. If there are discrepancies between the client's and the partner's reports of drinking or/and urges, follow these up. Do not assume one partner is the more accurate reporter. Simply comment on the fact that there is a discrepancy and ask each partner to explain why they wrote down what they did. These discrepancies provide an opportunity to clarify how the partner understands the client's actions (if she misinterpreted his behavior as indicating drinking when he didn't), and also provide an opportunity to emphasize the importance of honesty (if the partner reported drinking that the client hadn't written down).

Try to keep conflict low during this discussion and treat the discrepancy matter-of-factly. You may use the following sample dialogue:

> *It's not surprising that you have different perceptions—drinking often leads to problems with communication, discomfort with being honest, and a lot of guessing. That's one of the reasons I like to have both of you keep track—it helps to increase your communication and understanding of each other.*

The following exchange between partner (P) and therapist (T) provides an example of how to handle discrepancies in recording.

P: I didn't see him for a couple of days this week. I didn't know what to write down so I left the card blank for those days.

T: Can you make any estimate for those days? Did you talk to him on the phone, or did he tell you something about those days when you saw him? If so, please make your best estimate. If you honestly cannot even make a guess, you may have to leave it blank, but I would prefer that you write something down for every day. Even if you don't see each other, though, I would like you to do a rating of your satisfaction with your relationship.

Review the partner's homework to be supportive of the client's efforts to change, ask both partners how they felt about the homework, and discuss any adjustments that would make it more comfortable and helpful for both of them. Ask the partner to continue efforts to be supportive in the coming week.

Collect the completed DPQs from the client and the partner. Check each item for completeness, and have them fill in any missing items. Tell them that you'll be using the DPQs later in the session.

Graphing Progress
Alcohol Use and Urges

Use the blank Alcohol Use and Urges Graph provided to graph data from the client's self-recording cards. You may photocopy the graph from the book if necessary. The client can complete his or her own blank graph in the workbook as well.

The following three data points should be graphed immediately on a graph where the X-axis is time (the baseline and 12 sessions):

1. Total number of standard drinks consumed for the week (add up the number of drinks)

2. Total number of urges during the week (urge frequency) (count up the number of urges)

3. Average strength of urges during the week (1–7) (add up the ratings for all the urges during the week and divide by the total number of urges)

An example of a completed Alcohol Use and Urges Graph is shown in Figure 5.1.

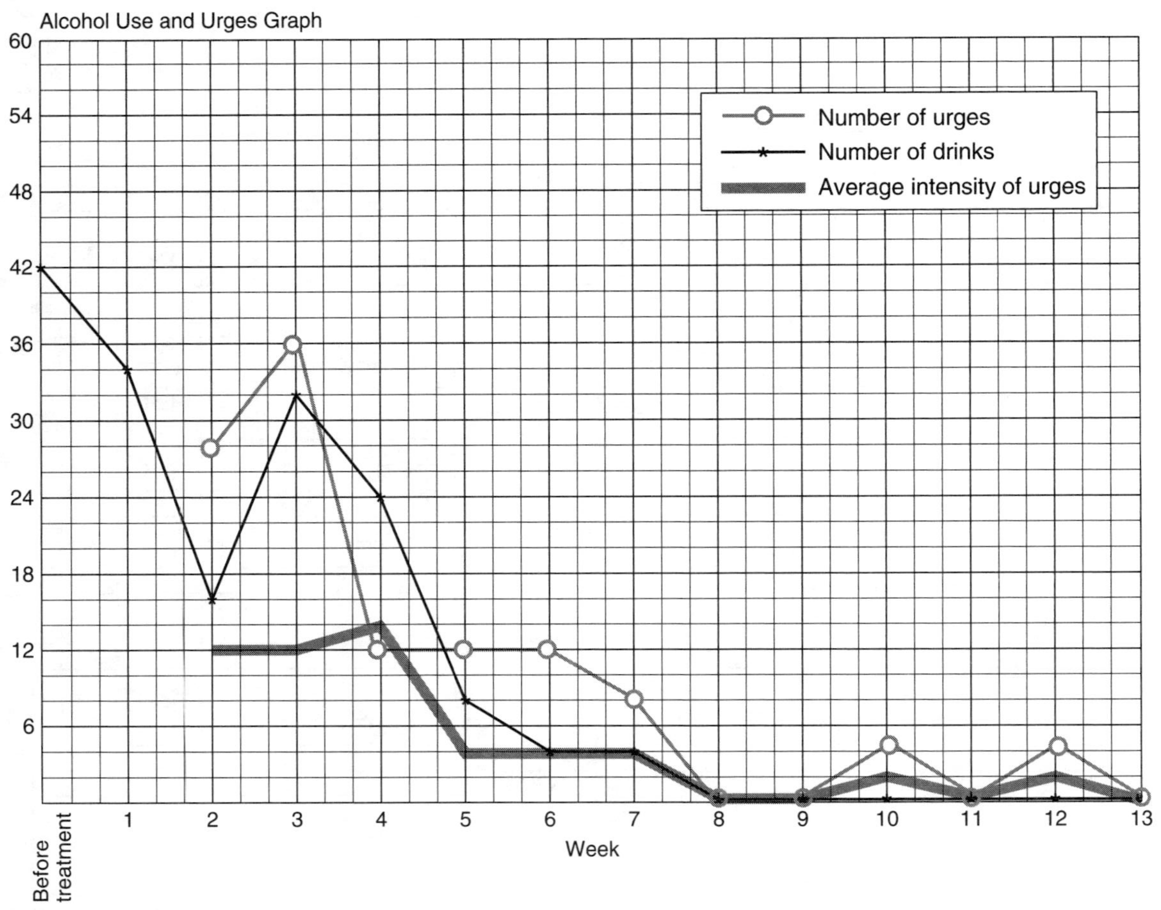

Figure 5.1

Example of Completed Alcohol Use and Urges Graph

Alcohol Use and Urges Graph

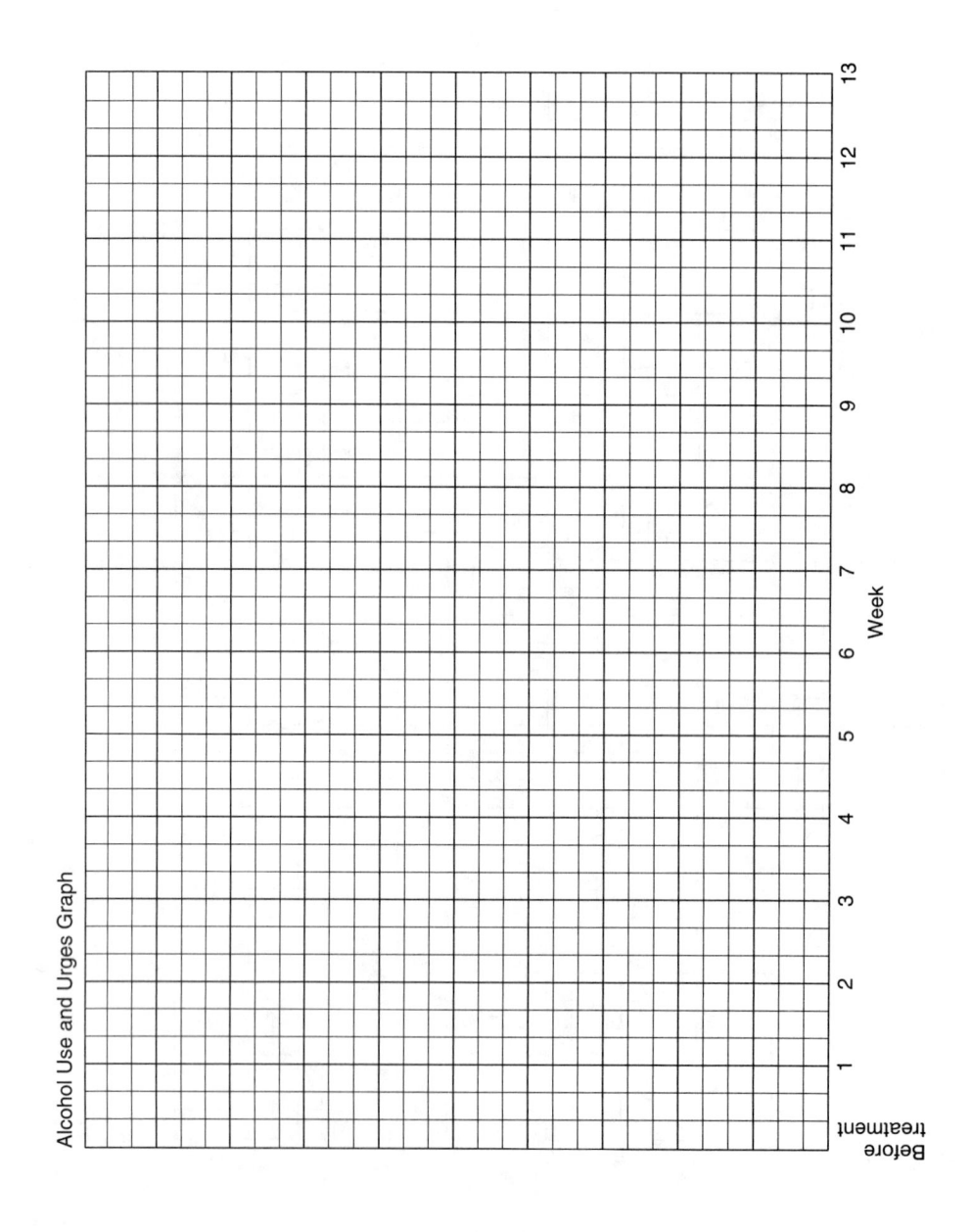

Before treatment | Week 1 2 3 4 5 6 7 8 9 10 11 12 13

Relationship Satisfaction

Use the blank Relationship Satisfaction Graph provided to graph the couple's average relationship satisfaction for the week. Use different colors for the client's and his or her partner's lines. Again, you may photocopy the blank graph provided here as necessary. The couples can complete their own blank graph in the workbook as well.

Explain to the couples that graphing the data each week will help track progress.

An example of a completed Relationship Satisfaction Graph is shown in Figure 5.2.

Check In (10 min)

Ask the couple how their week was in general. Acknowledge both partners' concerns. Use information from this discussion for specific topics in the rest of the session. Review with the couple the basic format of each session. Point out that you cannot cover everything at once, that treatment will go step-by-step, that treatment is a process, and that by the end of the 12 sessions they will have acquired a whole new set of skills to become and remain abstinent from drinking and to get along better.

Check in on and discuss progress of abstinence plan. Update the plan if necessary.

Functional Analysis (35 min)

Explain to the client that learning to identify situations that trigger drinking and learning to cope with them will help him or her feel better about staying sober. Discuss functional analysis (habit analysis) as the first step in understanding and gaining self-control over "out-of-control" drinking. Tell the client that problem drinking is a habit triggered by certain cues and maintained by both long- and short-term "maintainers" or consequences.

It is important that the partner also understand the functional analysis, as future sessions will focus on aspects of his or her behavior that

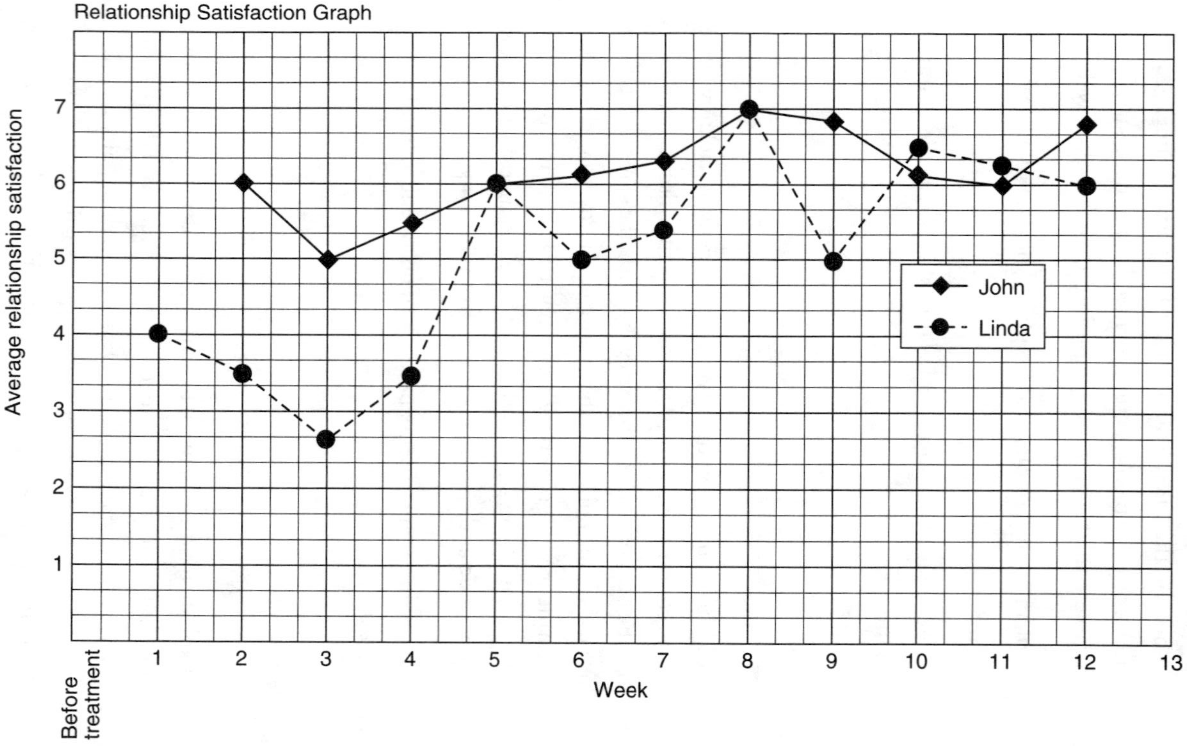

Figure 5.2
Example of Completed Relationship Satisfaction Graph

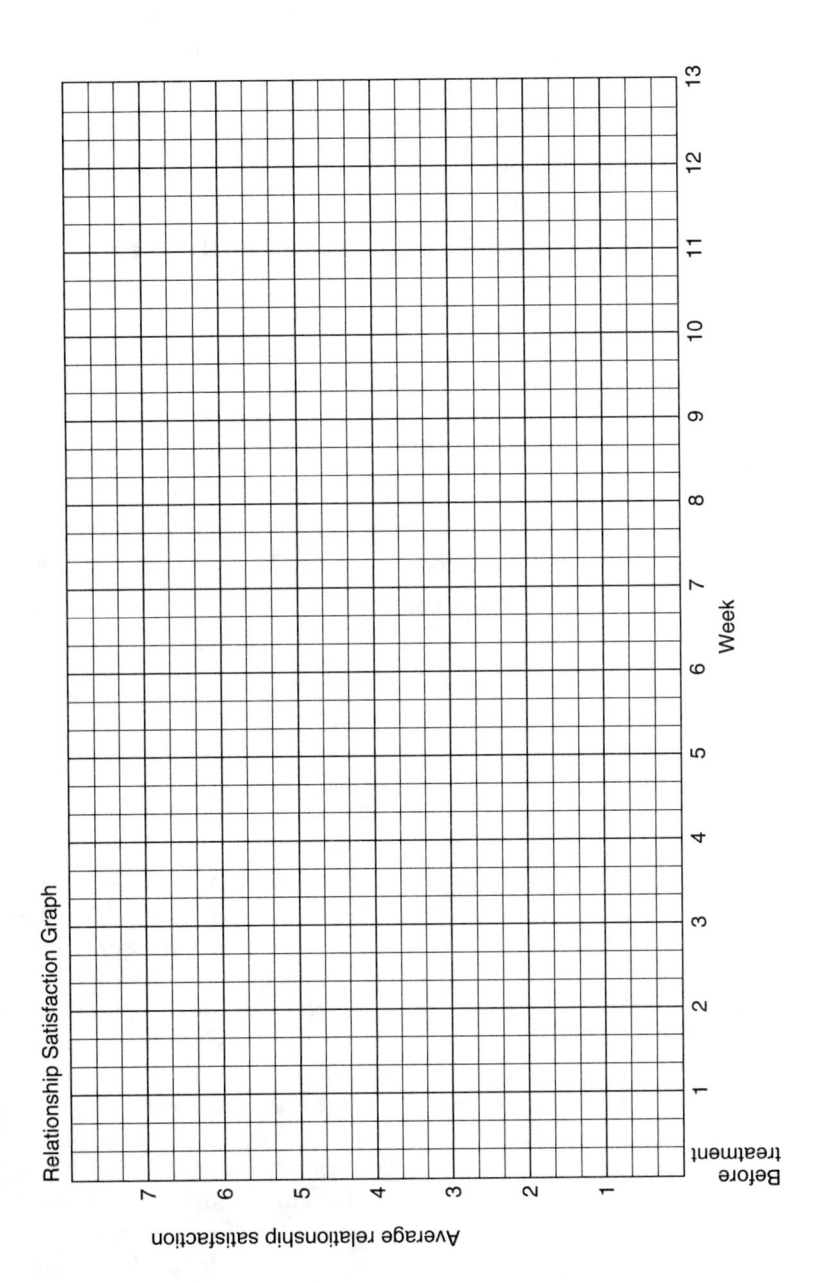

Relationship Satisfaction Graph

	Before treatment	1	2	3	4	5	6	7	8	9	10	11	12	13

Week

Average relationship satisfaction (1–7)

either serve as triggers for drinking or provide positive consequences for drinking. Include the partner in the initial explanation of the functional analysis by making eye contact and asking if he or she understands the concepts. As you explain that triggers do not *cause* drinking but rather *increase a drinker's desire to drink*, be sure to note that this is true for the partner's actions, as well as other events in the client's life. You should also review the partner report version of the DPQ to see if he or she described specific high-risk situations that are different than or in addition to those reported by the drinker. Take note of these additional situations, and ask the client whether he or she also viewed these situations as triggers.

Present the following rationale to the client:

> *The first step in achieving abstinence is understanding more about your drinking. Together we will carefully identify and analyze all the factors that seem to be high-risk situations for drinking. Then we will put it all together to come up with a plan that will work for you. This is called a **functional analysis** or a habit analysis. A functional analysis can be broken down into different steps. Let's look at each step of the chain* (review the steps as outlined in Table 5.1).

Table 5.1 Steps to Functional Analysis

Triggers	People, places, and things will be associated with drinking. A trigger is something that usually occurs before drinking. A trigger can be something easy to see or something sneaky. Often the drinker is not aware of the triggers. Triggers don't make people drink; they just set up thoughts and feelings connected to drinking.
Thoughts and Feelings	Triggers set up thoughts and feelings. The triggers bring up feelings and ideas that are connected to drinking. These thoughts and feelings can be nice or unpleasant. Some examples are "I need to drink to be more sociable," "People will think I am weak if I don't drink," "Drinking will help me relax," or "Drinking will make me happy."

continued

Drink	Drinking is something you do. It is a behavior that is a part of the chain.
Positive Consequences	Very often something nice happens when someone drinks. The alcohol will often cause pleasant feelings. People learn to expect that alcohol will make them more relaxed, more sociable, or happier. These pleasant effects help keep people stuck on alcohol.
Negative Consequences	The trouble that comes with alcohol often comes later. The trouble comes in many forms: arguments in the family, problems with a boss, financial difficulties, poor health, etc. Because the trouble comes later on, many people don't always make the connection between the trouble and their drinking. Many times, the possible trouble is out of your mind when thoughts of the pleasant parts of drinking are on your mind.

Refer the client to Chapter 2 of the workbook for more information on functional analysis. Also refer the client to the sample behavior chain in the workbook and discuss using the following dialogue:

For example, say it's 5 pm on Friday and you've had a long week at work. Your co-workers are going out to Happy Hour at a sports bar that you pass on the way home. They've asked you to join them. You figure you might as well stop for a quick drink and you'll still be home in time for dinner, since you've had such a tough week and you deserve a short break. At the bar, you get involved with conversation; your co-workers order you a second and then a third drink, and by the time you arrive home it's 8 pm, you've had four drinks, missed dinner and your spouse is pretty angry.

In this example, **first***, it being Friday afternoon and your co-workers inviting you out—after a tough week that left you tense—happened* **before** *you drank and "set the stage" for drinking. We call these* **"triggers"**— *risky situations, places, people, times, or feelings that lead up to your drinking. They happen before you drink—they trigger or create a desire to drink (Ask if client understands or has* questions.) *Triggers are like yellow or red traffic lights; they signal "Danger—trouble coming up ahead unless you stop."*

Second, *triggers are usually associated with certain thoughts and feelings. Feelings in this example would be tension, fatigue, and anticipation of relaxing. Examples of thoughts are, "I deserve a short break from my routine. I'll just stop for one drink and stay 30 minutes."*

Third, *starting to drink and beginning to feel relaxed from a few drinks all happen during or just after drinking and then you couldn't stop at 1 or 2 drinks. These things are also important and go on during or after drinking itself. They are* **positive consequences**. *These can be short- or long-term.*

Fourth, *staying late and missing dinner at home, which causes your spouse to be angry, are* **negative consequences** *of drinking; they happen as a result of drinking. These can be short- or long-term.* (Ask if the client has any questions or comments.)

This whole series of events is called a **behavior chain** *(of triggers, thoughts and feelings, drinking behaviors, and consequences):*

Review the following steps for completing a functional analysis based on the preceding example.

1. *First you write in the "Drink" column when and where the drinking happened. In our example, the person had four drinks at the sports bar Friday evening.*

2. *Then think back to what happened before the drinking happened. What were the people, places, or things that set up the drinking? Write these things in the "Trigger" column. In this example, the person had had a tough week and co-workers invited him out to a sports bar. Friday at 5 pm was also a trigger.*

3. *After writing the triggers, think back to those thoughts and feelings that made drinking more likely. In this example, the person thinks about being tired and tense after the work week, feels he deserves a break, and anticipates relaxation and fun at the bar.*

2 Trigger feelings	3 Thoughts and	1 Drink When/(Where?)	4 Positive consequences	5 Negative consequences
Friday 5 pm, invitation from co-workers to go to sports bar	Tired and tense. "I deserve a break. I'll just have one quick drink and go home"	At sports bar Friday evening—stayed 2 1/2 hours, had 4 drinks instead of 1	Relaxation, initial euphoria from alcohol, socialize with friends, fun	Stayed too long, drank too much, spouse angry (argument followed), didn't see kids, drove under influence, had a hangover the next day

Figure 5.3

Example of Completed Behavior Chain

4. After this, think about what happened after drinking. Remember the good things, the positive consequences. It is realistic to say that good things will happen, in the short term, to people when they drink. In our example, the person feels more relaxed, enjoys the initial euphoria from the alcohol, and enjoys socializing with his friends from work.

5. Now think about the things that happened later—the negative consequences. The problems created by drinking often come later on. In this example, the drinker had an argument with his wife, missed seeing his kids before bedtime, his driving was impaired, and he had a hangover the next day.

Figure 5.3 shows how the completed behavior chain for the preceding example would look.

As with most people, the person in this example falls into a pattern. Some triggers will set off thoughts and emotions that lead to drinking. The drinking leads to some nice things happening. These nice things encourage the drinker to keep using alcohol.

The functional analysis helps you learn about your patterns. Most people are not aware of the patterns and habits that happen in their lives, and it takes some detective work to identify them.

We will look at each part of the chain and find out what your patterns are and how to change them. That is what a functional analysis of your drinking patterns is all about. Now perhaps you can begin to see why we ask such detailed questions; we need to know precisely and exactly what your particular drinking patterns are like. Every individual is different. This is all part of the treatment.

The first part of gaining self-control of your drinking will be to analyze your drinking habits; the second part will be to learn ways to rearrange your environment (your triggers, drinking behaviors, and maintainers or consequences); the third part will be to learn positive alternatives to alcohol use (give examples of assertion or lifestyle balance); and the fourth part will be to learn how to maintain these changes. These four steps will help you gain self-control and maintain long-term abstinence.

Now let's start a list of all of your triggers (ask the client to turn to the List of Triggers worksheet in the workbook). *As you can see on the worksheet, triggers can be environmental, interpersonal, emotional, etc. Let's try to think of what some of your triggers are.*

Exercise—List of Triggers

Help the client list his or her triggers on the worksheet, using both partners' DPQs, self-recording cards, and intake information as guides. Look for the types of situations rated most highly on the DPQ as well as individual items. If the partner has listed different situations as high-risk, ask him or her to explain why these seemed particularly important. Then ask the client whether these situations should be added to the list of triggers and include them if he or she agrees.

Exercise—Behavior Chains

After the client has completed the List of Triggers, help him or her complete the Behavior Chain worksheet in the workbook.

When you and the client have worked out two behavior chains on the sheet, ask the client how he or she felt about the exercise, what stood out, and if there were any surprise reactions. Ask the partner if he or she has any thoughts or questions. Review the client's completed behavior chains to help him or her understand the various parts of the drinking chain triggers and consequences. Point out that there are both positive and negative consequences (give examples).

Choose several situations from the list of triggers and have the client work out at least 2 more behavior chains as homework for this week.

Noticing Positive Behaviors in Each Other ("Notice Something Nice")(20 min)

Explain that when couples have problems, they often get into the habit of focusing on the negative. They can list every bad or annoying things that their partner does, but either don't even notice the good things or just take them for granted. Or, they may see positive actions in a negative light, being suspicious of the other person's motives even when they do something good. Ask the couple if this scenario sounds familiar to them.

Therapist Note

■ *Some couples may start to focus on negative aspects of their partner. The therapist should not let negative comments go on, and can divert them by noting that their focus on the negative in the session underscores the need to notice the positives as well.* ■

Exercise—Notice Something Nice

Using the Notice Something Nice worksheet in the workbook, ask each partner to name something positive that they noticed the other person do this week. It might be something that happens every day, such as taking care with personal grooming, or bringing the other person a cup of coffee after dinner, or it may be something more unusual or special. Each partner should also be asked to name one thing that they did that they viewed as positive for the other or for the relationship. Again, this might be something routine like the husband filling up his wife's car

Notice Something Nice

1. Client — What nice things did your partner do this week?
   Told me I was beautiful
   Massaged my feet when I was tired
   Was nice to my daughter when she was visiting

2. Partner — What nice things did your partner do this week?
   Said she loved me
   Didn't complain about the past after my ex-wife called me
   Made us a nice dinner with all my favorite foods

Figure 5.4
Example of Completed Notice Something Nice Worksheet

with gas or the woman making dinner. Try to identify two to four positive behaviors to list for each of them. Figure 5.4 shows a sample Notice Something Nice worksheet.

For homework, ask the couple to use the back of their recording cards to write down one positive action that they notice from their partner each day during the week. They should not comment to each other about these actions but simply record them. You may use the following sample dialogue:

> *We've found that starting to focus on the positive can make a big difference. Just by seeing the good things each day and looking for good actions can help you view your partner and your relationship in a different light.*

> *Focusing on the positive doesn't mean you have no problems and it won't make all your problems go away. But, if you realize there's a lot of good in your partner and in your relationship, it's easier to face the problems as well.*

> *Each day, notice at least one good quality or action of your partner. Write it down. Don't tell your partner what you noticed, just keep track for yourself. We'll talk about them in the session.*

Anticipating High-Risk Situations This Week (10 min)

Work with the client to identify at least one high-risk situation coming up in the next week (see sample dialogue in Session 1). Have the client write out ideas for handling the situation on the High-Risk Situations worksheet in the workbook. Remember to include the partner in this discussion.

Homework (5 min)

- Instruct the client to continue self-recording and record coping with high-risk situations on the back of the client self-recording card.

- Ask the client to complete the List of Triggers and fill out 2 or more behavior chains on the Behavior Chain worksheet in the workbook.

- Instruct the client to take notice and record one positive partner action each day on the back of his or her self-recording card.

- Instruct the partner to continue recording the client's alcohol use and urges (intensity), and his or her own level of relationship satisfaction using the partner recording cards.

- Instruct the partner to continue supportive comments and actions.

- Ask the partner to notice and record one positive client action each day on the back of his or her recording card.

- Have the couple read Chapter 2 of the workbook.

Chapter 6

Session 3: High-Risk Hierarchy / Partner Functional Analysis Part I / Self-Management Plans

(Corresponds to chapter 3 of the workbook)

Materials Needed

- Copy of couple's workbook
- Breathalyzer and 2 tubes
- Client and partner self-recording cards
- Alcohol Use and Urges and Relationship Satisfaction graphs in progress
- High-Risk Hierarchy worksheet
- Partner-Related Triggers and Consequences worksheet
- Self-Management Planning Sheet
- High-Risk Situations worksheet

Outline

- Determine blood alcohol level (BAL) of both the client and his or her partner
- Provide overview of session (5 min)
- Review self-recording and homework (10 min)
- Check in (5 min)
- Continue with "notice something nice" (5 min)
- Work with client to develop a hierarchy of high-risk situations (15 min)

109

- Perform a functional analysis with the partner to determine triggers for drinking (20 min)
- Teach client how to create self-management plans for dealing with high-risk situations (20 min)
- Identify potential upcoming high-risk situations and plan for how to cope with them (5 min)
- Assign homework (5 min)

Blood Alcohol Level Determination

If the client's or partner's BAL is greater than .05, reschedule the session. If the client is still drinking, remind client of the abstinence plan and revise if necessary.

Overview of Session and Set Agenda (5 min)

Present today's topics and ask the couple if there are any additional issues they would like to discuss.

Review Self-Recording and Homework (10 min)

1. Collect and review the client's self-recording cards and discuss any questions and/or problems the client may be having. Reinforce the client for completing homework and making progress. Be sure to review the client's completed High-Risk Situations worksheet and discuss how he or she handled the situations.

2. Also collect and review the partner's self-recording cards. Note and discuss any discrepancies between client and partner reports of drinking and urges and resolve these. If the partner's report indicates more drinking and the client acknowledges the drinking, add this information in with the client's original self-report, and update the Alcohol Use and Urges Graph. Review and update the Relationship Satisfaction Graph, and note the similarities or

differences in how each partner is feeling about the relationship this week.

3. Check the client's completed functional analysis homework (Behavior Chain worksheet) and review both positive and negative consequences of the drinking of each situation recorded. For homework, ask the client to choose two times during the week when he or she experiences a "strong urge," and then develop all the triggers and thoughts about consequences around these two specific real-life events; that is, have the client develop two more complete behavior chains around actual urges recorded on his or her self-recording card. If client is not having "strong urges" have him or her use any two urges that seem important during the week.

4. Check that the partner is still providing support or encouragement to the client each week, and ask the couple how this has been working for them. Do not assign additional partner support homework, but encourage the partner to continue these actions as they feel comfortable.

Check In (5 min)

Ask couple how their week was in general. Acknowledge both partners' concerns. Use information from this discussion for specific topics in the rest of the session.

If introduced in Session 1, check in with the client on the success of the abstinence plan. If the client is still drinking, update the plan.

Continue with "Notice Something Nice" (5 min)

Review the couple's self-recording cards once again, and check to see if either partner wrote down any positive behaviors each may have noticed in the other. If there are positive behaviors noted, ask each partner about their experience with the exercise, and ask each one to tell the other what they wrote down. If they did not write down any positive behaviors, inquire about any difficulties the couple may have had with the exercise.

They will be assigned this same exercise for homework at the end of the session.

Developing a Hierarchy of High-Risk Situations (15 min)

In the last session, you discussed triggers and high-risk situations. Today, you will work with the client to plan for these difficulties. To make planning easier, ask the client to list potential problem situations in order from least difficult to handle to most difficult to handle. Present the following rationale to the client:

> *In the last session, we identified some of the major situations, feelings, people, and behaviors that are associated with your drinking. Doing this tells us what may make attaining or maintaining abstinence difficult for you. We need to plan for those difficulties. To make your planning easier, I recommend that you put your list of difficulties in order so that you can plan to tackle some of the easier problems and situations first.*

Refer the client to the section in Chapter 3 of the workbook entitled "Looking Ahead for Trouble." Review the information with the client using the copy provided on the following page.

Looking Ahead for Trouble

Smart travelers look ahead for possible trouble. By looking ahead for rough spots in the road, they can handle tough situations better. Travelers who see the trouble ahead on the road can make changes to steer around the problem. In the same way, people who quit drinking can look ahead for difficult situations. Smart people plan for the rough spots.

Everybody who has stopped drinking has faced people, places, or things that made it difficult to stay sober. Some situations are more difficult than others. For you, some situations will be easier to handle. Other situations will be more difficult to manage.

What are your rough spots? What people, places, emotions, or things can be trouble for you? Think of what goes with drinking:

- People
- Places
- Emotions, like sadness, anger, boredom, and happiness
- Events, like parties
- Things you see, like bottles
- Problems with your partner
- Problems with your children
- Good times

Some rough spots are harder and others are easier to handle. You can usually tell ahead of time how hard something will be. By thinking about how hard different situations can be, you can be ready for the tougher ones.

We want you to write down all your difficult situations. Try to think of anything that could get you feeling like drinking. Try to write them down in order, from the hardest to the easiest.

Then we want you to rate how hard each situation is for you. The easiest way to do this is by using numbers. Use numbers between 0 and 100 to describe each situation. Larger numbers mean that the situation is harder to handle. Smaller numbers mean that the situation is easier. Something that is no trouble at all would get a number 0. Something that would be very hard for you to handle would get a higher number. The number 100 would mean that the particular situation was the most difficult one for you to handle without drinking.

Exercise—High-Risk Hierarchy

Therapist Note

■ *This part of the session focuses primarily on the drinker, but you should encourage the partner to listen to the discussion, ask questions, and offer his or her perspective on what situations are more or less difficult for the drinker.* ■

Use the client's completed List of Triggers worksheet from Session 2 to create a hierarchy of high-risk situations. Add any new triggers to the list as necessary.

Ask the client if he or she believes that there are differences in how difficult these situations are to cope with without drinking. If the client says no, pick the most extreme ones, and ask if they are equally difficult. The client undoubtedly will say that there are some differences in difficulty. Introduce the High-Risk Hierarchy worksheet in the workbook. Suggest that each situation can be rated for difficulty, on a 0–100 scale, where 0 = extremely easy to cope with without alcohol and 100 = extremely difficult to deal with without drinking. Using the worksheet, write down

---

High-Risk Hierarchy

Difficult Situation

		How Hard?
		very easy — very hard
		0 - - - - - - - 100
1.	Being alone all day	100
2.	My partner won't talk to me	95
3.	Feeling sad; thinking no one cares about me	90
4.	My partner yelling at me	75
5.	Ex-wife won't let me see my son	50
6.	Fridays after work	20
7.	Beer commercial on TV; seeing someone else drinking	10
8.	Eating pizza	5

Figure 6.1

Example of Completed High-Risk Hierarchy

three triggers and ask the client to assign ratings to them. For homework, ask the client to put the situations in order from least to most difficult, and assign a difficulty rating to each. Figure 6.1 shows a sample High-Risk Hierarchy.

Partner-Related Functional Analysis (20 min)

Review the client's behavior chains and completed DPQ in preparation for this part of the session. In addition, use The Coping Questionnaire and the partner's version of the DPQ and make a list on a blank piece of paper of partner triggers and consequences. Use these, plus partner behaviors noted earlier, as the basis for developing a list of partner-related behaviors that directly impact on drinking—both as triggers and as consequences. Focus especially on those partner behaviors that are clearly part of the problem drinker's functional analysis. The partner functional analysis should include partner behaviors that seem to be triggers for drinking, as well as partner behaviors that may either reinforce drinking or protect the drinker from negative consequences of drinking. Protection from negative consequences may be a tricky concept for the partner to understand. Essentially, the partner should understand that the more the client experiences the full force of the bad effects of drinking, the more motivated he or she will be to change. As much as possible, we want the partner to stop protecting the drinker.

Present the following rationale to the couple:

> *Some high-risk situations for drinking may come from things that you (the partner) do. As I have emphasized before, you are not to blame for (the client)'s drinking, and he/she always has responsibility for drinking or not drinking. But, there are things that you may do that are triggers for his/her drinking—that is, they increase his/her desire to drink. You also react to (the client)'s drinking. Some of your reactions may protect him/her from experiencing negative consequences that otherwise would occur, while others may be positive consequences for drinking, even though you don't want them to be. Our goal first is to determine what actions of yours are triggers for (the client)'s drinking and how you might be protecting him/her or providing positive consequences for drinking. We've already been talking about some of*

these, but I'd like to come up with a more complete list. After we've done that, we'll start to identify which triggers and consequences you want to and can change, as another way to support (the client) *in staying sober.*

Let's go over some examples to show you what I mean. (Refer to the partner-related functional analysis information in Chapter 3 of the workbook.)

Case Example 1

Robert comes home from work and finds the kids playing unsupervised and Nancy lying on the couch drunk. He gets mad and yells at her and she goes upstairs to drink more. He makes dinner for the kids and then feels guilty for having yelled at his partner. He brings her dinner in bed.

In this example, Robert's complaining about irresponsibility because of drinking is a *trigger* for further drinking. This is a *partner-related trigger*. After drinking, *short-term positive consequences* for Nancy might include avoiding making dinner, not being bothered by the children, and getting served dinner in bed! *Long-term negative consequences* might include Nancy feeling depressed, guilty, and angry with herself for having no self-control over drinking and being lazy and not spending time with the children.

Figure 6.2 shows how the completed behavior chain for the preceding case example would look.

Trigger	Thoughts and feelings	Behavior	Positive consequences	Negative consequences
Robert calls me irresponsible.	He's right. I'm a horrible mother.	Drink alone, upstairs	Robert makes dinner. I have no responsibilities for a while.	Depressed, guilty, angry with myself. Robert is very angry.

Figure 6.2
Nancy's Behavior Chain

Case Example 2

Jane hasn't been drinking for about two months. John's company picnic is coming up and he suggests that they go. Jane doesn't know many people, and feels very uncomfortable there. They join up with a group of John's co-workers and their wives for dinner, and everyone is drinking beers or wine coolers. Someone offers Jane a wine cooler and she drinks it, and then three more. She feels upset and disappointed with herself, but on the way home, all John talks about is what a great time they had. She feels terrible and continues to drink after they get home.

In this example, John's taking Jane to the picnic was a trigger for drinking. His lack of awareness of her distress was a trigger for additional drinking. Positive consequences of drinking were that Jane felt like she was part of the group. Negative consequences include her disappointment with herself and her anger at John for being unaware of the difficulty she had had. Figure 6.3 shows how the completed behavior chain for the preceding case example would look.

Trigger	Thoughts and feelings	Behavior	Positive consequences	Negative consequences
Company picnic. Someone gives me a wine cooler. John's talking with his buddies.	Uncomfortable Angry at John What's the use?	Drink 4 wine coolers	Feel more comfortable at picnic.	Keep drinking at home Still angry Broke my sobriety John doesn't understand.

Figure 6.3
Jane's Behavior Chain

Use the following sample dialogue to summarize both case examples:

You can see from these examples that each man reacted in ways that seemed normal and understandable for the situation, but in each situation their actions led to their wives feeling bad and drinking more. You also know that in many situations it's hard to know what to do. Our first task, though, is just to identify actions of yours that may be triggers. In the coming sessions, we'll talk about what to do.

Exercise—Triggers and Consequences

Using the Partner-Related Triggers and Consequences worksheet in the workbook and the list you prepared before the session, introduce the following exercise using the sample dialogue provided.

Now let's look at some of the ways you might "trigger" or provide positive consequences for your partner's desire to drink. I looked over the questionnaire you filled out earlier, and also the DPQs that you and your partner completed. I started to make a list of some actions that might be triggers or positive consequences, but we should complete this list together.

To start, figure out which actions of yours might trigger your partner's desire to drink and add these to the list we created earlier. You can ask your partner for input if you feel comfortable.

Think about the ways you have protected your partner in the past—by taking care of your partner when he or she was drinking, by covering up for your partner with friends or family, by picking up your partner's responsibilities, etc. Add these to the list.

Think about ways you might have provided positive consequences when your partner drank—by having a few drinks with him or her, having a good time at a party or with friends and letting your partner know it was fun, or by trying to be nice and not make waves when your partner was drinking. Add these to the list.

In later sessions, we'll talk about ways to change, as well as the actions that you don't want to change.

Start with the list of partner coping behaviors from the Partner Feedback Sheet (Session 1) and additional behaviors noted from The Coping Questionnaire that might be triggers. Show the partner the list, and ask the partner and the client if any of these might be triggers or consequences. Those that both partners agree are triggers, protections, or consequences should be entered on the triggers and consequences worksheet.

Partner-Related Triggers and Consequences

Actions of mine that might be triggers for *Frank's* drinking:

Being in a bad mood

Refusing to talk to him when something's bothering me

Bringing up the past

Actions of mine that might be positive consequences for *Frank's* drinking:

Being nice to him when he's been drinking

Joining him in fun activities when he's been drinking

Being physically intimate with him when he's been drinking

Actions of mine that might protect *Frank* from the consequences of drinking:

Calling his boss to say he's got the flu when he's too drunk to go to work

Tiptoeing around the home when he had been drinking the night before

Taking care of him when he's hung-over

Figure 6.4

Example of Completed Partner-Related Triggers and Consequences

Ask the client for input as well, focusing particularly on how partner behaviors become triggers for him or her (thoughts and feelings). Ask the partner to think of other actions that relate to his or her partner's drinking, and have the partner complete the worksheet (listing triggers and consequences) as homework. Figure 6.4 shows a sample.

It may be necessary to give the couple a taste of couple therapy during this discussion. You can briefly make couple interventions during these sessions and note what principles are involved so that these principles can be consolidated in the subsequent couple sessions. It is sometimes therapeutic simply to label a problem clearly and in a non-judgmental way.

Therapist Note

- *There are many types of partner triggers; they may include some or all of the following:*

  - *Partner drinking*
  - *Partner offering alcohol to the client*
  - *Partner attempts to control the client's drinking (either directly or through threats and other negative behaviors)*
  - *Negative or critical partner comments related to drinking*
  - *Other negative or critical partner comments*
  - *Relationship conflicts about topics unrelated to drinking*
  - *Partner involving the client in a tempting drinking situation that he or she wouldn't have to face if not for the partner*

Self-Management Plans (20 min)

Therapist Note

- *Although self-management planning is an individual intervention, you should occasionally turn to the non-drinking partner during the explanation and exercise, ask if he or she has any additional ideas, and ask for general input or feedback during the exercise.*

Present the following rationale to the client:

> *We have discussed your drinking as a habit triggered by certain cues and maintained by certain consequences, but knowing about triggers isn't enough. We need a plan! Developing a good plan takes patience and a lot of thinking. We have a step-by-step method that makes planning much easier. We are now going to focus on those cues/events/triggers and begin to come up with ways to rearrange and change them so as to make life less risky.*

Training in "stimulus control" procedures is aimed at teaching the client to alter the antecedent triggers for drinking that have been identified, with the result of decreasing the likelihood of drinking in response to these cues. This means thinking of ways to rearrange those environmental events that used to trigger drinking or replacing them with non-risky situations. The antecedents were identified through the DPQ, self-recording, functional analysis, and high-risk hierarchy exercise. Focus on settings or situations, times, and people. Naturally, these categories are related to each other and several can be going on at the same time. For some clients only a subset of these antecedents will be applicable.

Explain that external environmental events often can trigger drinking. Divide environmental events into categories (time of day/week, settings, persons, situations). Give examples and relate these to the DPQ and functional analysis (after work, weekends, while watching TV advertisements, when others are drinking). There are three basic ways of handling these environmental antecedents differently to reduce the risk of drinking. Discuss them with the client using the following dialogue:

> *One way is to remove yourself from the environment (e.g., not going out with your friends or your partner to a party or a bar). This may involve coming up with alternative things to do or places to be to avoid those times, places, people that are problematic.*
>
> *Another way is to rearrange the environment (e.g., don't keep alcohol in the house in a highly visible place; don't carry money with you if you have to walk right past your favorite liquor store).*
>
> *A third way is to behave differently in the same environment, by using different coping skills.*

In deciding how to handle these situations, the client may want to consider how to change his or her overall lifestyle—does the client want to work longer hours, spend more time with family, begin to exercise, pursue a hobby, learn something to further his or her career or just for pleasure, etc. While most clients will not yet have a clear idea of what they want, they should be encouraged to think about their overall lifestyle when developing self-management plans.

Exercise—Self-Management Planning

Review and explain the sample Self-Management Planning Sheet in Chapter 3 of the workbook. When the client understands the exercise, pick a salient trigger from his or her completed High-Risk Hierarchy and develop a self-management plan for the particular trigger. Review the following instructions from the workbook with the client. Use them to help the client develop a plan for managing triggers.

1. Pick out triggers that you will come across soon. Start with an easier trigger. As you get more practice at this, you can plan for harder triggers.

2. Write down as many ideas as possible for handling the trigger. Be creative! Do not worry about being silly or unrealistic. The best ideas often come when you let ideas fly without stopping to think about what is good or bad about each one. The evaluation will come later. There are three kinds of strategies for handling triggers:

    1. Remove yourself from the situation to avoid trouble.
    2. Change things around you to avoid the trigger. For example, get rid of alcohol around the house or do not walk past the liquor store.
    3. Think or act in different ways when you are faced with the trigger. For example, someone may avoid drinking by remembering the consequences that will come later.

3. *After* coming up with a lot of ideas, think and write down what is good and bad about each one. Now is the time to think about what you need to do for each one of the ideas. Remember, some consequences of your plan will happen quickly and others will happen later. Try to think them through. The goal here is to think about what is good and bad about each idea.

4. Think about how easy or hard each idea would be for you. Some ideas will be hard to do, others will be easy. For each idea or plan, give it a number between 1 and 10 that shows how hard it would

be to do. For example, the easiest plan that you can do would get a 1. The hardest thing that you could ever do would get a 10. Write down how hard each idea would be for you. That is, how difficult would it be to carry out the new plan in place of old behavior that involved drinking in response to the same trigger?

5. Pick a plan. Choose the plan or plans that have the best balance between positive and negative consequences. Try to pick ones that will not be too hard for you.

6. After putting a plan to work, check to see how it is working. If a plan is not working, do not be afraid to make changes or to pick another idea.

If time in session is short, work with the client to choose at least two of his or her triggers and complete steps 1–4 for each. Figure 6.5 shows a sample Self-Management Planning Sheet.

Self-Management Planning Sheet

Trigger	Plan	+/−Consequences	Difficulty (1−10)
After work on Friday	Go to the gym	+ Will feel healthy − Too tired to work out	5
	Have a romantic night with my partner	+ Will get to spend quality time with each other − My partner may not be interested	6
	Go to an AA meeting	+ Will get support − Will get home pretty late	2
	Work from home on Friday	+ Less pressure than being in the office − Not practical to do every week	8

Figure 6.5
Example of Completed Self-Management Planning Sheet

Anticipating High-Risk Situations This Week (5 min)

Work with the client to identify at least one high-risk situation coming up in the next week (see sample dialogue in Session 1). Have the client write out ideas for handling the situation on the High-Risk Situations worksheet in the workbook. Remember to include the partner in this discussion.

Homework (5 min)

- Instruct the client to continue self-recording and record coping with high-risk situations on the back of client self-recording card.

- Instruct the client to create a hierarchy of high-risk situations, with ratings of difficulty in handling.

- Have the client complete a self-management plan for 2 trigger situations.

- Ask the client to identify two times during the week when he or she experiences a "strong urge" to drink and complete a behavior chain for each one. If the client is not having "strong urges," have him or her use any two urges that seem important during the week.

- Ask the client to notice and record one positive partner action each day on the back of the self-recording card.

- Instruct the partner to continue recording the client's alcohol use and urges (intensity), and his or her own level of relationship satisfaction using the partner recording cards.

- Instruct the partner to notice and record one positive client action each day on the back of the partner recording card.

- Ask the partner to complete the Partner-Related Triggers and Consequences worksheet.

- Have the couple read Chapter 3 of the workbook.

Chapter 7

Session 4: Partner Functional Analysis Part II / Enhancing Motivation to Change

(Corresponds to chapter 4 of the workbook)

Materials Needed

- Copy of couple's workbook
- Breathalyzer and 2 tubes
- Client and partner self-recording cards
- Alcohol Use and Urges and Relationship Satisfaction graphs in progress
- Self-Management Planning Sheet
- Alcohol in the House Plan worksheet
- Decisional Matrix worksheet
- High-Risk Situations worksheet

Outline

- Determine blood alcohol level (BAL) of both the client and his or her partner
- Provide overview of session (5 min)
- Review self-recording and homework (5 min)
- Check in (5 min)
- Review "Notice Something Nice" homework, and ask each partner to give the other feedback once during the week about one positive action they had written down (5 min)

125

- Complete functional analysis of partner-related patterns (20 min)
- Continue discussion of self-management plans, including Alcohol in the House Plan (20 min)
- Introduce the Decisional Matrix and work with the client to enhance motivation for treatment (20 min)
- Identify potential upcoming high-risk situations and plan for how to cope with them (5 min)
- Assign homework (5 min)

Blood Alcohol Level Determination

If the client's or partner's BAL is greater than .05, reschedule the session. If the client is still drinking, remind client of the abstinence plan and revise if necessary.

Overview of Session and Set Agenda (5 min)

Present today's topics and ask the couple if there are any additional issues they would like to discuss.

Review Self-Recording and Homework (5 min)

1. Collect and review completed recording cards from both the client and the partner and use the data to update the Alcohol Use and Urges and Relationship Satisfaction graphs. Reinforce the couple for compliance. Add any relevant information (i.e., antecedent–consequent conditions) to functional analysis sheet.

2. Consider questions, problems regarding client functional analysis homework.

3. Review client's high-risk hierarchies. Discuss any situations that the client did not rate. Evaluate client's ratings to see if there appear to be any major discrepancies between what you believe are

the client's difficulties with coping and his or her ratings. Explain to the client that he or she will continue to select problems from these hierarchies to work on.

4. Briefly review the self-management plan homework and put it aside to use later in the session.

Therapist Note

▪ *Review of "Notice Something Nice" and "Partner Functional Analysis" homework should be completed during the part of the session devoted to each topic.* ▪

Check In (5 min)

Ask the couple how their week was in general. Acknowledge both partners' concerns. Use information from this discussion for specific topics in the rest of the session.

If introduced in Session 1, check in with the client on the success of the abstinence plan. If the client is still drinking, update the plan.

"Notice Something Nice" and Feedback (5 min)

After reviewing the "Notice Something Nice" homework, ask each partner to give the other feedback once during the week about one positive action they had written down.

Complete Functional Analysis of Partner-Related Patterns (20 min)

Last week, you asked the non-drinking partner to create a list of his or her own triggers, positive consequences, and protection behaviors for the client's drinking. Review this list and make additions if necessary. Briefly relate this list to the client's already completed behavior chains.

Review the partner's completed behavior chains and obtain agreement from the couple that relevant triggers and consequences have been identified. Emphasize cooperation. Add in any partner-related behaviors that are identified by the client but which the partner was unaware of. Also take note of behaviors identified by the partner that the client is not aware of. Use the elements of surprise, blame, or denial positively in terms of relief that a "hidden pattern" has come up and what both people can see can now be dealt with effectively and cooperatively. Continue to label and remind clients about obvious areas of relationship conflict.

State that both client and partner-related functional analyses are now completed and remind couple about the rationale for having this information (learned habit, individual responsibility regardless of what partner is doing, controlling yourself is controlling your environment). The analysis can be changed or added to, and encourage clients to bring up new problems whenever they become aware of them.

> *The first step is completed, becoming aware of all the components that relate to drinking or not drinking. This is all part of treatment to help change things. Based on this detailed understanding of your unique patterns, in the remaining sessions, we will focus specifically on different parts of the chain and work together to identify alternatives for both of you to make abstinence easier and more rewarding.*

Continuation of Self-Management Planning (20 min)

At this point in the session, you will review the client's completed Self-Management Planning Sheet in more detail.

Exercise—More Self-Management Planning

Help the client choose another example from the High-Risk Hierarchy, the one rated as more difficult, and work out a self-management plan for that trigger. For homework, have the client complete a Self-Management Planning Sheet for all triggers not yet covered.

Alcohol in the House Planning

Most of the self-management planning done up to this point has focused on the drinker only. However, certain topics affect both partners, and the couple should learn to address these situations together. A simple example is deciding what to do about keeping alcohol in the house. There is no universal, "correct" solution, but the couple should talk together to develop a solution that is correct for them.

Present the following rationale to the couple:

> *One type of situation that partners are often concerned about is having alcohol in the house. Some partners would like to keep alcohol in the house to be able to have an occasional drink herself or to serve when company is over. Other times, a partner will be concerned that the stocked liquor cabinet, or beer in the refrigerator, is just too much of a trigger for drinking. Some problem drinkers feel similarly; others find that alcohol in the house does not make much difference. Have the two of you thought about this? Have you discussed it with each other at all?*

Exercise—Alcohol in the House Plan

Using the Alcohol in the House Plan worksheet in the workbook, have the couple discuss this topic with each other for a few minutes, trying to come to a decision about how they will handle alcohol and the house. Help them follow good listening and communication skills. Encourage each of them to express their own feelings about whether or not to keep alcohol in the house, to make positive suggestions for solutions, and to compromise. You may need to have each partner paraphrase what the other is saying to assure that they understand each other. It is important that the client not agree to anything that he or she feels will jeopardize his or her ability to stay sober. Work toward an initial agreement that both partners can live with and have them implement it during the week. Have the couple write down their plan on the worksheet. A sample plan is shown in Figure 7.1.

Alcohol in the House Plan

1. We will get rid of any alcohol that's in the house by throwing it away. We'll do it together.

2. When we have friends over, we won't serve any alcoholic drinks.

3. If someone brings alcohol as a gift, we'll say, "Thank you, but we don't drink so please keep it."

4. If guests bring alcohol for themselves to drink, we will allow them to drink, but will make sure that they take any leftover alcohol home with them. If they forget, we will dump out the remaining alcohol and throw the container away after they leave.

Figure 7.1
Sample Alcohol in the House Plan

Decisional Matrix and Motivation Enhancement (20 min)

This part of the session focuses primarily on the drinker. However, the partner often has very clear perspectives about positive and negative consequences of drinking and of abstinence. First, ask the drinker for his or her thoughts about what to put down in each part of the Decisional Matrix in the workbook and then ask the partner for additional suggestions. Ask the drinker if he or she agrees before writing something down that the partner suggested. It is important that the drinker have the final say because the matrix should reflect his or her views. If you believe that the partner's contribution is valid but the drinker disagrees, record the partner's comment in brackets along with his or her name/initials.

Present the following rationale to the client:

> *Even though you have entered treatment, you probably have some mixed feelings about being in therapy and about actually making major changes in your life. This is a common feeling. You don't know what things will be like in the future, and that makes it somewhat frightening. In contrast, you do know what things are like now. Sometimes the familiar is comforting, even if it is unhappy. You are*

also giving up something that has provided good things in your life. Most people get pleasure from drinking—they enjoy the taste, like the sensations, and associate it with many good things in their lives. Giving it up is like saying good-bye to a friend you will miss, even though we both know that alcohol is not a friend with your best interests in mind. Having mixed feelings about giving up alcohol is perfectly natural.

You may also have mixed feelings about abstinence. Some people feel that it's impossible to have fun without alcohol or feel that it's the only way they can relax.

Exercise—Decisional Matrix

Introduce the Decisional Matrix exercise using the following dialogue:

I'd like to help you think out some of the pros and cons of drinking and not drinking. In thinking about the pros and cons, it may be helpful to think about short-term consequences and long-term consequences.

Review the following information from the workbook with the client.

The Good, the Bad, and the Ugly of Drinking

Think about what things happen when you drink. We call these things consequences. Some consequences are good, others are bad. Most of the time, the good consequences happen right as you are drinking. The bad consequences come later.

There are reasons why you drink. These come from the good things that happen, even if the good things only happen sometimes. Your mind and body remember these things.

The bad consequences can come right when you are drinking (like getting sick or having a fight) or can come later (like not being able to get up the next morning or having your children upset with you).

It will be easier to quit if you have a list of the bad things about drinking. The more you remember the bad things, the easier it is to say no when you have an urge to drink.

Also think about what will be good and bad about quitting drinking. Some people don't think ahead when they make a change in their life. You will be more successful if you look ahead to see the good and bad about making a change. Thinking about what you lost and what you get makes it easier to stay motivated.

Take a moment and start writing down the things that happen to you when you drink. Write down the things that happen right away and the things that happen later. Some kinds of consequences are:

- Physical things: body sensations or effects like getting sick
- Negative feelings
- Depressing thoughts
- Things that happen with other people, such as family or friends
- Money or legal trouble
- Work problems

On the Decisional Matrix sheet, write down the good and bad things that happen right away (immediate consequences) when you drink. Also write down the good and bad things that happen later (delayed consequences) after drinking. Write these in the row marked "Continued Alcohol Use."

Do the same thing for quitting drinking. Write down the good and bad things that will happen right away when you stop drinking. Then, write down the good and bad things that will come later. Write these in the row marked "Abstinence."

Be realistic! It is important to be honest. The more we understand the reasons why you drink, the easier it will be to find a solution. When we are done, we want to have more good reasons for stopping drinking than for keeping things the way they are.

Ask the client whether or not he or she can relate to these comments, and encourage discussion. After some general discussion, ask the client to identify some good and bad things about drinking. Have the client write these down on the Decisional Matrix in the workbook. Also ask the client to think of some pros and cons of abstinence. Have the client write these down on the worksheet as well. A sample Decisional Matrix is shown in Figure 7.2.

For homework, ask the client to spend more time on this exercise and fill out the worksheet as completely as possible.

Decisional Matrix

Abstinence

Pros (short- and long-term)	Cons (short- and long-term)
Stay alive	Hard to be in my skin
Get along with my partner better	Will miss drinking
My children will respect me more	May experience withdrawal symptoms
I will respect myself	

Continued alcohol use

Pros (short- and long-term)	Cons (short- and long-term)
Makes me feel better, bad feelings go away	I could lose my job
Good way to get even with my partner when we're fighting	I could lose visitation with my children
Allows me to let loose and have a good time	I could become physically violent
	I will probably fight with my partner more
	I may experience blackouts
	I could end up in the hospital
	I could become severely depressed

Figure 7.2
Example of Completed Decisional Matrix

Anticipating High-Risk Situations This Week (5 min)

Work with the client to identify at least one high-risk situation coming up in the next week (see sample dialogue in Session 1). Have the client write out ideas for handling the situation on the High-Risk Situations worksheet in the workbook. Remember to include the partner in this discussion.

Homework (5 min)

- Instruct the client to continue self-recording and record coping with high-risk situations on the back of the client self-recording cards.

- Have the client complete self-management plans for triggers not yet done.

- Have the client complete the Decisional Matrix.

- Have the client implement self-management plans and write on back of self-recording cards how triggers were dealt with.

- Instruct the client to continue recording positive things about his or her partner and giving feedback once during the week.

- Instruct the partner to continue recording client's alcohol use and urges (intensity), and his or her own level of relationship satisfaction using the partner recording cards.

- Instruct the partner to continue recording positive things about the client and giving feedback once during the week.

- Have the couple implement a plan for either keeping or not keeping alcohol in the house.

- Have the couple read Chapter 4 of the workbook.

Chapter 8

Session 5: Dealing with Urges / Decreasing Partner Triggers

(Corresponds to chapter 5 of the workbook)

Materials Needed

- Copy of couple's workbook
- Breathalyzer and 2 tubes
- Client and partner self-recording cards
- Alcohol Use and Urges and Relationship Satisfaction graphs in progress
- Dealing with Urges worksheet
- Coping with Urges—Partner Role worksheet
- Partner Self-Management Planning Sheet
- High-Risk Situations worksheet

Outline

- Determine blood alcohol level (BAL) of both the client and his or her partner
- Provide overview of session (2 min)
- Review self-recording and homework (5 min)
- Check in (10 min)
- Discuss ways of dealing with urges to drink (15 min)
- Discuss ways in which the partner can be helpful when the client experiences urges to drink (10 min)

- Talk about ways of decreasing partner triggers for drinking (20 min)
- Review skills and progress made thus far (20 min)
- Identify potential upcoming high-risk situations and plan for how to cope with them (5 min)
- Assign homework (3 min)

Blood Alcohol Level Determination

If the client's or partner's BAL is greater than .05, reschedule the session. If the client is still drinking, remind client of the abstinence plan and revise if necessary.

Overview of Session and Set Agenda (2 min)

Inform couple of topics that will be covered in the session. Ask the couple if there are any additional issues they would like to discuss today.

Review Self-Recording and Homework (5 min)

1. Collect and review completed recording cards from both the client and the partner and use the data to update the Alcohol Use and Urges and Relationship Satisfaction graphs. Reinforce the couple for compliance.

2. Review the client's completed High-Risk Situations worksheet. Determine if there were any situations that the client did not anticipate, and see if he or she could have anticipated these ahead of time. Reinforce successful coping.

3. Review decisional matrix homework. Ask the client to discuss his or her reactions to the decisional matrix homework and whether or not it had an impact on his or her desire to be in treatment or to change.

4. Check that the client has completed self-management plans for two more triggers from the High-Risk Hierarchy. Assign two more for the week from higher-risk situations on the hierarchy.

5. Review implementation of a plan for keeping (or not keeping) alcohol in the house.

6. Review "Notice Something Nice" and feedback homework.

Check In (10 min)

Ask couple how their week was in general. Acknowledge both partners' concerns. Use information from this for specific topics in rest of session.

By Session 5, the client should be completely abstinent from drinking. If not, we suggest the following interventions:

1. Check client's motivation for abstinence by revisiting his or her Decisional Matrix and reasons for seeking treatment (see Session 4)

2. Remind client that this is an abstinence-based treatment and revise the abstinence plan

3. Identify the situations in which the client is drinking

4. Identify what is getting in the way of quitting

5. Help client choose a target quit date

6. Help client identify ways to prepare for the target quit date

7. Assess the level of physical dependence. Does the client need a supervised detoxification or higher level of care?

8. Consider an alternate drinking goal

Dealing With Urges (15 min)

Explain to the couple that as the client tries to cut down or stop drinking, he or she will experience urges to drink. In this section, you will offer the client some ways to handle these urges.

Ask the following questions to help the client articulate his or her own beliefs about urges, and counter these beliefs where appropriate. Occasionally you should solicit the non-drinking partner's views. You may use the following sample dialogue:

> *I'd like to discuss your understanding of urges to drink by asking you some questions, and then we'll work on ways to help you cope with urges. First—where do you think that urges come from?*

Try to help the client view urges *as responses to external situations that are difficult to cope with (i.e., triggers).* Probe for the belief that urges are physiologically based or are caused by lack of motivation to change, and help the client and partner understand the relapse prevention model of urges, which emphasizes situational cues and coping deficits.

> *Second—what do you think it means if you are experiencing urges?*

Try to help the client view urges as signs of the need to cope with a situation differently, not a sign of addiction.

> *Finally—what has your experience been with urges? When you do experience an urge to drink, how long does it last? What happens to the intensity? Does it keep getting worse and worse, or does it get better over time?*

Elicit the client's beliefs about the time course of urges. Does he or she view them as time-limited or as something that will continuously increase in intensity over time unless he or she drinks?

Address the partner:

> *Sometimes partners worry that urges mean that the drinker isn't serious about changing or is sure to relapse. Have you had those concerns?*

Solicit the partner's views.

Continue the discussion by reviewing with the client the important points to remember about urges and triggers.

> *Urges are reactions to triggers. Your body has learned to connect certain people, places, and things to drinking. The triggers can even be thoughts or emotions. Urges are a sign that you have to do something different. Something in the situation is making it difficult for you.*

The way you handle the situation has to change. Urges to drink don't last forever! They are like waves in the ocean—they peak, they crest, and they subside. They usually go away in a short time. Even though the few minutes can seem very long, remember that the desire to drink will go away if you give it time.

To summarize, emphasize with the client and partner that urges can be seen as:

1. triggered by external events;

2. a natural experience associated with change;

3. an indication of the need to cope differently with a trigger;

4. time-limited; and

5. not an indicator of motivation or prognosis—almost everyone has urges when they stop drinking

Exercise—Ways to Deal With Urges

Discuss with the couple the various ways of effectively coping with urges to drink. You may use the following sample dialogue:

There are many effective ways to cope with urges. Some people cope best through thinking, some through action, and some through contact with other people. Let's talk about some of these options.

You might find that the use of imagery is a helpful way to deal with urges. We have found that different clients experience urges differently and that different images help them. For some clients, the best way to deal with urges is to "go with the flow"—that is, to recognize and accept the urge and just ride it out. Other people find that they want to use active imagery to deal with urges. Which of these views seems more like your feelings about urges?

Ask carefully about the client's views here, in order to develop the best imagery. Select imagery consistent with the client's preferred mode of thinking about urges. For clients who select the mode of actively dealing with urges, an image that Marlatt and Gordon (1985) suggest is that of the Samurai—viewing the urge as an enemy, that, as soon as recognized, is "beheaded."

Other images are of a wine glass filled with bleach, or a wine glass with a dead spider floating at the bottom, or an older woman or man sitting alone at a bar, drunk, face weathered and lined, eyes glazed, or any other negative image that is meaningful. These images are only examples. The client might come up with another image that he or she finds more compatible.

Explain to the client that some people prefer to deal with urges through activity. Ask the client to identify a couple of other approaches to handling urges that may be useful. The client may think that getting involved in a distracting activity can help him or her deal with urges to drink. Reading, working on a hobby, going to a movie, and exercising (jogging, biking) are all good examples of distracting activities. Once the client gets interested in something else, he or she will find that the urges go away in no time. Another effective response to craving is eating, as most people don't feel like drinking after eating a big meal or something sweet. Instead of a drink, the client can have a sugarless hard candy and a glass of iced tea or iced seltzer with juice. Or, when attending a buffet or function where there is an open bar, the client can begin immediately with some hors d'oeuvres and a glass of soda with ice.

Explain to the client that some people cope best with urges by reaching out to other people. Ask the client if there are people he or she could call who would distract from an urge (i.e., someone the client likes to talk to) or who could help him or her deal with an urge (i.e., someone who understands what the client is trying to do). Summarize the discussion for the client using the following sample dialogue:

> *In summary, here are some ways of dealing with urges to drink. Pick one or more that will work for you.*
>
> - *Remind yourself that the urge is a temporary thing. No matter how bad it is, it will not last forever.*
>
> - *If possible, get away from the situations that created the trigger.*
>
> - *Go through the list of reasons why you decided to stop drinking. Remind yourself about the bad parts of drinking. Remind yourself about the good things about not drinking.*

- *Find something to do that will get your mind off the urge to drink. A fun activity that does not involve drinking will help distract you from the struggle.*

- *Talk with somebody who will understand. Often just talking about the urge will take some pressure off you.*

- *Say encouraging things to yourself that will make you feel good about not drinking.*

- *Another way to use your imagination is to have a picture in your head of the urge looking like an ugly monster. Think of yourself as a ninja or a samurai fighting back and beating the monster. Or picture bleach poured in a wineglass.*

- *Imagine that you are in a boat and the urge is a big wave that comes and rocks the boat, but then passes you by.*

- *Tell yourself you can't always control when an urge comes, but you can just accept that "there's that urge again," and let it stay until it evaporates. Don't try to get rid of it, just kind of ignore it, distract yourself, and it will go away eventually.*

- *And, last but not least, you can pray.*

Have the client write down ideas for dealing with urges on the worksheet provided in the workbook.

Partner Role in Dealing With Urges and Urge Discussion (10 min)

Present the following rationale to the couple:

Sometimes, it is helpful to talk about an urge with someone else. Many times, talking with your partner may help you sort out what is triggering the urge or may help you think of something to do that will help you get over the urge.

Without discussing it ahead of time, it is often hard for a partner to know how to be helpful. Sometimes, a partner might be afraid that an urge means that you are going to drink. Sometimes the partner might feel that it is wrong to have urges.

Address the couple:

Have the two of you ever tried to discuss (the client)*'s urges to drink? If so, what happened?*

Exercise—Dealing With Urges Together

Using the Coping with Urges—Partner Role worksheet and the information in Chapter 5 of the workbook—have the couple talk about ways the partner could be helpful when the client has an urge to drink.

Examples that couples have come up with in the past include:

- offering to make a cup of coffee or tea and sit down and talk
- going for a walk together
- asking the client what's triggering the urge

You may use the following sample dialogue with the partner:

Remember, urges are a normal part of stopping drinking. Urges are reaction to triggers. Urges do not mean that your partner is a failure, will drink, or will not be successful. They simply mean that your partner needs to cope with his or her triggers.

Your partner is learning many ways to cope with urges and you can help. Ask your partner how you can help. Sometimes you can help by listening. Sometimes there is something you can say that will help—just ask! Sometimes there is something you can do. You can get your partner a soft drink or a cup of tea or you can go for a walk together.

You may feel anxious or angry when your partner has an urge to drink. Remind yourself that urges are normal. Take a deep breath and calm yourself if you need to. Keep your eye on your goals of a sober partner and a happier family.

Emphasize positive communication skills, such as listening, asking how to help, or offering concrete suggestions that they had talked about previously. See if the couple can come up with at least two ways that the partner could respond that would be helpful. Record these on the worksheet in the workbook. The couple may also identify actions of the partner that would not be helpful. If so, record these on the worksheet as well. Role-play one scenario in the session. For homework, have the couple practice at least one urge discussion during the week.

Decreasing Partner Triggers for Drinking (20 min)

Present the following rationale to the partner:

In the last sessions, we developed a list of some of the things you do that are triggers for your partner's drinking. Now, we're going to look at some of these to see which ones you think you might try to change. We'll use the same self-management approach we did with your partner—we'll look at a specific trigger, brainstorm ideas about what you might do differently, weigh out the pros and cons, think about how difficult this change might be for you, and then pick an approach. Let me show you an example of how self-management planning might work for you.

Here are the basics:

Write down as many ideas as possible for changing how you handle a specific situation. Be creative! Don't worry about how good the idea is.

Look at the pros and cons of each idea. Think about how comfortable you are with the idea, if it would help reduce the trigger, and if there'd be a "cost" that you won't like.

For each idea, think about these pros and cons, and rate how difficult it would be for you to carry out each idea.

Pick a plan. Choose the plan or plans that seem to have the best balance of positives and negatives.

Put your plans into action and see how they work.

Therapist Note

■ *Self-management planning with the non-drinking partner is a bit more complex than with the drinker, because the partner's self-management plans need both to decrease the trigger for the drinker and be behaviors that the partner is willing to engage in. As the partner brainstorms for alternatives and assesses the pros and cons of each, check in with the client to see if these ideas would be helpful. The alternatives must be acceptable to the partner as well.* ∎

You may use the following sample Partner Self-Management Planning Sheet (Figure 8.1) to illustrate the partner self-management approach to changing his or her behavior.

Trigger	Plan	+/− Consequences	Difficulty (1–10)
Ordering a bottle of our favorite wine in a restaurant	Order a glass just for myself	+ I enjoy the wine	2
		− My partner has to see me drink	
	Ask my partner if she's comfortable with my ordering wine	+ We'd be communicating	3
		− My partner may be uncomfortable and I won't get to drink	
	Order a different alcoholic beverage	+ My partner would be more comfortable	2
		− The drink may still serve as a trigger	
	Order a non-alcoholic beverage	+ I'd be supporting my partner	5
		− I might feel resentful	
Giving my partner very limited amounts of money so she won't spend it on liquor, which makes her feel bad and increases her desire to drink	Give my partner money for the week	+ It's what I normally do	9
		− I will be fearful that my partner will use the money for alcohol	
	Tell my partner that I'm worried she will use the money for alcohol	+ Feels good to be honest	5
		− Will hurt my partner's feelings	
	Give my partner enough money for a couple of days and increase the amount based on my partner's ability to stay sober	+ I will worry less	2
		− My partner may feel like I'm treating her like a child	
	Give the money to my partner's mother to manage	+ I wouldn't be the "bad guy"	10
		− My partner would be very upset	

Figure 8.1

Example of Completed Partner Self-Management Planning Sheet

Exercise—Partner Self-Management Plan

After reviewing the examples, work with the non-drinking partner to select one partner trigger and develop a self-management plan for it using the blank sheet provided in the workbook. Be sure to involve the client, particularly in generating alternatives and discussing their pros and cons. For homework, the partner should work up self-management plans for two more partner triggers.

Review of Skills and Progress (20 min)

This is a chance to catch up on interventions not delivered yet, and to provide a time for you and the couple to review and reflect on material covered thus far, to evaluate the client's progress toward the goal of abstinence, to reflect on positive aspects of the couple's participation and the positive consequences of their behavior change. Also, ask about areas that are still difficult and problematic for the couple and discuss those as challenges to address during the rest of the therapy.

The review should cover skills related to the client's drinking, partner-support behaviors, partner insight into effective and ineffective ways he or she has coped with the client's drinking, and enhancing awareness of the positive aspects of their relationship.

Refer the couple to the section "Look How Far You've Both Come" in Chapter 5 of the workbook and review the skills covered in treatment up to this point. The section highlights skills already learned as well as upcoming treatment topics. A copy for your use is provided on page 146. Use this discussion to point out how much progress has been made.

> *Let's review this handout together to highlight your progress over the past few weeks, as well as the new skills you've learned. The handout also lists the topics we have yet to cover as part of the treatment program. This is to give you the "big picture" of the treatment plan and to help you see how much progress you've made here and how many new skills you now have under your belt.*

Look How Far You've Both Come

For the Client:
You already have learned a great deal in treatment. You have been practicing many skills to help keep you from drinking. You have been doing self-recording, learning to recognize your triggers, and gaining insight into the behavior chain that leads to drinking after one of your triggers is pulled. You've learned what cues in the world around you may start you feeling and thinking your way toward drinking. You've figured out which risky situations are going to be the toughest for you, and since forewarned is forearmed, now you can be prepared. And you have learned to see well ahead of time that these situations are coming up, so now you can plan accordingly. You'll see the trouble before you are right on top of it!

You've learned to generate plans for dealing with triggers so that you are prepared with a specific way to deal with each one. You have considered the pros and cons of drinking and of abstinence so that you may feel more strongly that the pros of abstinence outweigh the pros of drinking. You are also clearer on the cons of drinking. You have some new tools to deal with urges and cravings.

For the Partner:
You've learned a lot about what your partner is doing to deal with her drinking problem. Understanding more about drinking and how to change can make it easier for you to support your partner. You've been keeping track of your partner's drinking and urges and understand more about what triggers are hard for your partner to handle. You've also learned about your own actions—the things you do that make it easier or harder for your partner to stay sober. Now we're starting to think about how to change your actions. And you've been focusing on being supportive—giving your partner the encouragement she needs to face this difficult problem.

For the Couple:
You've just started building a better relationship. You've started to notice nice things that your partner does and are learning how to express your appreciation for those nice things.

You've started to learn how to talk together to solve problems related to drinking, what to do about having alcohol in the house, and how to work together when drinking urges occur. You're well on your way!

Later on in the program, you'll both be learning to create more rewards for sobriety to replace the positive consequences of drinking, recognize the negative consequences of drinking, challenge thoughts about alcohol that get you into trouble, deal effectively with situations where alcohol is present, make safer decisions, share more enjoyable activities, communicate with each other more effectively, solve problems, identify warning signs that could lead to relapses, and avoid relapses and deal with any slips.

Anticipating High-Risk Situations This Week (5 min)

Work with the client to identify at least one high-risk situation coming up in the next week (see sample dialogue in Session 1). Have the client write out ideas for handling the situation on the High-Risk Situations worksheet in the workbook. Remember to include the partner in this discussion.

Homework (3 min)

- Instruct the client to continue self-recording and record coping with high-risk situations on the back of the client self-recording cards.

- Instruct the client to complete two more self-management plans for more difficult items on the High-Risk Hierarchy.

- Instruct the client to use urge coping twice during the week in a high-risk situation or another time when experiencing an urge.

- Instruct the couple to practice at least one urge discussion during the week.

- Instruct the partner to continue recording client's alcohol use and urges (intensity), and his or her own level of relationship satisfaction using the partner recording cards.

- Ask the partner to develop two self-management plans for his or her triggers for the client's drinking.

- Have the couple read Chapter 5 of the workbook.

Chapter 9

Session 6: Rearranging Behavioral Consequences / Shared Activities

(Corresponds to chapter 6 of the workbook)

Materials Needed

- Copy of couple's workbook
- Breathalyzer and 2 tubes
- Partner and client self-recording cards
- Alcohol Use and Urges and Relationship Satisfaction graphs in progress
- Decisional Matrix from Session 4
- 3 × 5 index card
- Partner List of Protecting from Drinking Worksheet
- Ideas for Enjoyable Activities Worksheet
- Alternatives to Drinking Worksheet
- High-Risk Situations worksheet

Outline

- Determine blood alcohol level (BAL) of both the client and his or her partner
- Provide overview of session (5 min)
- Review self-recording and homework (10 min)
- Check in (5 min)

- Help the client rearrange behavioral consequences by increasing positive thoughts about staying sober and negative thoughts about drinking (30 min)

- Encourage couple to engage in shared activities as a way to improve their relationship (15 min)

- Discuss ways the partner can stop protecting the client from the negative consequences of drinking (15 min)

- Identify potential upcoming high-risk situations and plan for how to cope with them (5 min)

- Assign homework (5 min)

Blood Alcohol Level Determination

Reschedule if BAL of client or partner is greater than .05. Check on compliance with homework and abstinence goal.

Overview of Session and Set Agenda (5 min)

Inform couple of topics that will be covered in the session. Ask the couple if there are any additional issues they would like to discuss today.

Review Self-Recording and Homework (10 min)

1. Collect completed self-recording cards from both the client and the partner and use the data to update the Alcohol Use and Urges and Relationship Satisfaction graphs. Reinforce the couple for compliance.

2. Review self-management homework. Both the client and the partner should have rearranged/avoided at least 2 triggers. For homework, have the client complete two more self-management plans, selecting items that are rated higher on the high-risk hierarchy (rated 50–75).

3. Review urge coping homework and ask the client if he or she found it helpful. Ask client if there are other skills to deal with urges that he or she thinks could be helpful. Instruct client to use these skills twice this week in urge or high-risk situations.

4. Review urge discussion homework and ask the couple if they found it helpful. Problem solve for any difficulties encountered. Encourage the couple to have another urge discussion during the week.

5. Review partner's self-management planning sheets and discuss any difficulties encountered. For homework, instruct the partner to implement an alternative to one of his or her behaviors that is a trigger for the client's drinking. The partner should also complete two more self-management plans.

Check In (5 min)

Ask couple how their week was. Acknowledge both partners' concerns. Use information from this for specific topics in the rest of the session.

If client is not abstinent at this point, discuss possible need for higher level of care.

Rearranging Behavioral Consequences (30 min)

Therapist Note

■ *During the discussion of rearranging behavioral consequences, focus primarily on the client, but include the partner in the psychoeducational aspects of the material. Enlist the partner's input both in the listing of negative consequences of drinking and in identifying alternative sources of reinforcement.* ■

Present the following rationale to the client:

> *Today we will talk about ways to increase the positive rewards you experience from staying sober. We are also going to discuss other ways to increase the positive thoughts that you have about staying sober and*

increase the negative thoughts that you have right now about drinking. We'll also talk about ways that you (the partner) can get out of the middle of protecting your partner so that he or she is even more certain that drinking will have negative effects.

Remind the client of the Decisional Matrix developed in Session 4. Turn back to the client's completed matrix in the workbook, and look at it together (or use a photocopy).

Now that the client has been in treatment two more weeks, it makes sense to update and change the matrix in any ways necessary. Ask the client to think of any additions that he or she would make to any parts of the matrix (short-term or long-term consequences of drinking or of sobriety). The goal of this session is to teach the client how to rearrange the consequences so that he or she thinks more clearly and convincingly about the negative consequences of drinking and learns how to reward him or herself with positive consequences for sobriety.

Now that we have reviewed some of the pros and cons of stopping versus continuing to drink, let's talk about two ways you can use this decisional matrix to help you become (stay) sober.

Thinking Through the Drink

First, I'd like you to practice thinking about the negative consequences of drinking before you drink. That is, just before you take a drink, you probably have been thinking mostly about the short-term pros of drinking, such as (point out the short-term positive consequences of drinking from the client's completed decisional matrix). *This exercise will help you start getting used to thinking about the cons of drinking, rather than the pros. This is one way of controlling your thoughts to help you avoid drinking.*

List negative consequences of drinking on a 3 × 5 index card, and then devise ways to increase the amount of time the client thinks about these consequences—the client must learn a new thinking habit. Have client read the 3 × 5 card prior to high-frequency activities (hang card on mirror in bathroom, put near coffee pot, in car, etc.). Consider the following example.

> *Some friends call and invite you and your partner to join them and a few other people at a club to relax and socialize. Your first thoughts will most probably be related to the positive consequences (don't be surprised, you have had a long time to develop that thinking habit). Delay accepting their offer ("I need to check my schedule, let me get back to you in an hour") and review your 3 × 5 card; practice your new thinking habit. Then call back and decline, using these suggestions:*
>
> *Be firm but polite—make it clear that you mean what you say when you decline.*
>
> *Suggest an alternative—Even though you aren't going to go to the club, say you'd like to see them and you wonder—would they like to come over for dinner on Sunday?*
>
> *We'll look at how to refuse drinks and drinking opportunities like this in depth in Session 8 in a couple of weeks.*

Increase the Positive Rewards of Sobriety

Look over the positive consequences of drinking that the client listed on the Decisional Matrix and present the following rationale.

> *Despite the negative consequences of drinking, we have to remember that the positive consequences are what kept you drinking, and giving up those positive aspects of drinking is difficult. When people develop a drinking problem, they experience the "funneling effect": many resources—time, money, energy, attention—are directed toward alcohol, including thinking about alcohol, getting alcohol, drinking, being drunk, and recovering from alcohol's effects.*
>
> *When people leave drinking behind, they often experience a frightening emptiness in their lives—the time and energy that drinking took has to be filled with something rewarding to keep you from going back to drinking, Try to think of it like this: One advantage of not drinking is that you have newfound freedom to use*

your time and resources in new ways, in whatever ways you choose. Let's make that a conscious choice. Let's think of ways to replace some of the positive consequences of drinking with rewarding activities that will be fun, positive, and healthy. To help you with that we've listed some activities in your workbook that many people enjoy

Refer client to the list of activities in the workbook. A copy for your use is provided on the following page.

What Do Other People Do?

Read a book together	On a rainy day, clean the house together	Play games with your kids at the park
Put on music and dance together	Sort through old photos and start a scrapbook	Take a long walk on the boardwalk
Go out for a nice meal	Make funny faces at each other	Explore all the parks in your county
Do volunteer work	Go "treasure hunting" at garage sales on the weekends	Go to a free lecture at the local community college
Go to a county fair	Work backstage or build sets for your local community theater group	Do yard work together
Play cards or board games	Give each other massages	Take your dog to the park
Shop for new furniture for your home	Call an old friend who lives far away	Paint a room in your home
Begin a knitting or carpentry project	Go to a sporting event	Sign up for a cooking class or art course
Go to a concert or play	Go to a museum or art gallery	Visit the zoo or aquarium
Go on a picnic	Lounge by the pool, weather permitting	Go on a camping trip
Take a bike ride	Order in and watch a DVD	Go horseback riding
Buy different flavored donuts, taste them all, and rate them	Run errands together	Have a "sex" date
Take a dance or martial arts class	Go into the city and window shop	Pray together
Plant a vegetable garden	Catch fireflies	Take a shower or bath together
Plant flowers	Make dinner together	Plan a trip someplace new
Join a book club	Go rollerblading	Volunteer at your local place of worship

Alternatives to Drinking

Discuss with client the notion that some of the positive consequences of drinking, such as euphoria and relaxation induced by alcohol, are not easily replaced but that these consequences were artificial and temporary, followed by the negative consequences.

Review the client's list of positive consequences of drinking as outlined on the Decisional Matrix, and develop a list of responses that serve as positive, rewarding alternatives to drinking (e.g., relaxation, social activities, enjoying nature). Go slowly and have the client record alternatives on the Alternatives to Drinking worksheet in the workbook. Remind the client to select alternatives that fit with his or her long-term goals. For example, the client might decide to go running or engage in another form of exercise to relax instead of reading or listening to music, if one of his or her long-term goals is to get into better shape. A sample Alternatives to Drinking worksheet is shown in Figure 9.1.

Alternatives to Drinking	
Trigger situation and positive consequences of alcohol	Alternative activity with similar positive consequences
Saturday night at a restaurant with your partner. Positive consequences of alcohol—relaxation, wine goes with dinner, euphoria, festive atmosphere	Get your favorite takeout food, eat at home, and then go to a movie
Tuesday night, partner working late, and no one is home. Positive consequences of alcohol—reduced loneliness, special time alone, relaxation	Join a gym and go swimming Tuesday night. On way home, stop at coffee shop or local bookstore
Friday, after work, doing yard work. Positive consequences of alcohol—relaxation	Stop at gym after work for an exercise class. Do the yard work Saturday morning instead
Neighborhood picnic, 4th of July. Positive consequences of alcohol—festive atmosphere, chance to be social, euphoria	Go to the gym before the picnic. Bring your own soda to the party. If there are too many tempting triggers at the picnic, leave

Figure 9.1

Example of Completed Alternatives to Drinking Worksheet

Shared Activities (15 min)

Begin the discussion of shared activities with the following:

In addition to the positive alternatives you're selecting as an individual, let's talk about ways to increase positive alternatives for you as a couple. We have begun to improve your relationship by helping you each notice positive things that your partner is doing. Clearly, dealing with the drinking and supporting changes in drinking are important aspects of getting along better.

Another way to improve your relationship is to simply share more positive activities together. Regardless of whatever else is going on, a couple can always come up with a block of 1–2 hours to do something pleasant together. All couples get stuck in routine ways of living together and feel there is nothing new or exciting to look forward to. Planning a new pleasurable, shared activity or reviving an old one and agreeing to be positive to each other can be satisfying. You both can agree to put aside everything else that's going on and do something that you both will find purely enjoyable.

Exercise—Planning Activities

Using the Ideas for Enjoyable Activities worksheet in the workbook, ask the couple about an activity that they would like to share during the week. If they have difficulty thinking of an activity, refer them back to the list of suggestions in Chapter 6 of the workbook to help them select an activity. Be sure the activity selected is something both partners will enjoy. Help the couple plan the specifics; including the day and time they will engage in the shared activity. Be certain to address practical issues that are relevant to the couple, such as costs, transportation, and childcare.

Partner-Changing Consequences (15 min)

Present the following rationale:

So far, we've been talking about ways that you (the client) *can rearrange the consequences of your drinking or sobriety yourself.*

Partners often try to protect the drinker from the consequences of drinking. The result is that the drinker does not experience negative consequences that would help motivate him or her to quit. The protection helps maintain the drinking. For example, you (the partner) *may shield the drinker from the embarrassment of having the children see him or her in a drunken condition. You may call your partner's boss and make excuses for absences. You may lie to family and friends to hide the drinking problems.*

One common type of protection is to give comfort to the drinker who is suffering from the effects of a drinking episode. Many partners will care for the "sick" person. Instead of suffering the full consequences of the drinking, the drinker gets special attention.

Partners protect the drinker for many reasons. Out of love, they do not want the drinker to suffer. They also do not want the drinking to affect other family members, particularly children. In many situations, the partner wishes to protect the drinker's job because it is an important source of money for the family.

The partner who protects the problem drinker is denying the drinker a full and true knowledge of his or her own problem. When you protect the drinker, you are not giving these powerful negative consequences a chance to work. The protection unintentionally helps keep the drinking going.

We've already made a list of some of the ways that you (the partner) *protect* (the client)*. You can help* (the client)*'s sobriety by coming up with changes that do not protect him or her from the long-term negative consequences of drinking.*

There are several important principles to remember as you think about trying to decrease or stop protecting (the client)*:*

1. *People change when what they do causes them too much pain;*

2. *Families often protect people with drinking problems from bad things that could happen when the person drinks;*

3. *Some protection is because families don't want to see the drinker suffer; some of the protection is because the family would also suffer if the negative consequence occurred (such as loss of income).*

You (the partner) *can identify what kinds of protection you think are appropriate to change and what actions you are not ready to change.*

Exercise—Partner-Changing Consequences

You may use the following sample dialogue to introduce the exercise:

You should agree together as a couple not to protect the drinker. If the drinker has a future slip, you (the partner) *should refuse to do any special favors for him or her. This means no hiding, no making excuses, and no caring for your partner when he or she is sick from drinking. It was the drinker's responsibility for drinking and it is also the drinker's responsibility to cope with the consequences.*

Make an agreement about what you (the partner) *will do if your partner slips. The agreement should say that your partner is responsible for the consequences if he or she drinks. You should not try to make the consequences any easier.*

It is important to plan and practice for the possibility of a slip. Think of possible situations that may occur between you. Talk about how you will act. You should imagine how you will handle the situation.

Think of a likely situation and go over in your imagination all the things that would likely happen in the particular situation. Imagine how you (the partner) *will firmly tell your partner that you will not make things easier for him or her. Rehearsing your reaction will make it easier to act at the right time.*

Using the Partner List of Protecting from Drinking worksheet and the section in Chapter 6 of the workbook entitled "Stop Protecting the Drinking," go over the list of ways that the partner protects the drinker from the negative consequences of drinking. Select one or two situations that aren't strongly emotionally laden. Help the couple discuss and reach agreement on a new behavior pattern that results in having the problem drinker take direct responsibility for his or her drinking and experience the *full negative consequences*. Choose relatively *low-level, non-emotional* behaviors such as telling a friend that he or she is sick and can't come to the phone when he or she actually has been drinking. Be prepared to respond to resistance, such as "If I don't do this, she won't love me; I would embarrass her; I cannot allow this to happen." Be empathic, but also help the partner see how his or her actions may help to perpetuate the drinking, and that if the client knows he or she won't be protected he or she will have more motivation to avoid drinking. Sometimes, the client can provide feedback about the value of experiencing some consequences. Obtain agreement from couple that it is OK to implement these changes. For homework, instruct the partner to make a list of new, "non-protective" reactions for each of the protection behaviors listed during the partner functional analysis. Suggest that the partner do this on his or her own and leave discussion and negotiation of more emotionally-charged changes for the next session.

Anticipating High-Risk Situations This Week (5 min)

Work with the client to identify at least one high-risk situation coming up in the next week (see sample dialogue in Session 1). Have the client write out ideas for handling the situation on the High-Risk Situations worksheet in the workbook. Remember to include the partner in this discussion.

Homework (5 min)

- Instruct the client to continue self-recording and record coping with high-risk situations on the back of the client self-recording cards.

- Instruct the client to continue to implement self-management plans.

- Ask the client to complete the Alternatives to Drinking worksheet in the workbook and practice two alternatives this week.

- Instruct the client to hang a 3 × 5 card listing negative consequences of drinking in at least one spot this week and read it on a daily basis.

- Ask the couple to practice at least one urge discussion during the week.

- ✎ Instruct the partner to continue recording client's alcohol use and urges (intensity), and his or her own level of relationship satisfaction using the partner recording cards.

- ✎ Remind the partner to implement an alternative to one of his or her behaviors that is a trigger for the client's drinking.

- ✎ Instruct the partner to develop two self-management plans for his or her triggers for the client's drinking.

- ✎ Ask the couple to carry out one shared pleasurable activity together.

- ✎ Have the partner make a list of new, non-protective reactions for each of the protection behaviors listed on the Partner List of Protecting from Drinking worksheet in the workbook.

- ✎ Have the couple read Chapter 6 of the workbook.

Chapter 10 | Session 7: Dealing With Alcohol-Related Thoughts / Communication Part I

(Corresponds to chapter 7 of the workbook)

Materials Needed

- Copy of couple's workbook
- Breathalyzer and 2 tubes
- Partner and client self-recording cards
- Alcohol Use and Urges and Relationship Satisfaction graphs in progress
- Planning for More Enjoyable Activities worksheet
- Dealing With Alcohol-Related Thoughts worksheet
- Strengths and Weaknesses in Our Communication worksheet
- High-Risk Situations worksheet

Outline

- Determine blood alcohol level (BAL) of both the client and his or her partner
- Provide overview of session (5 min)
- Review self-recording and homework (5 min)
- Check in (5 min)
- Help the couple plan shared activities for the next few weeks (10 min)

- Dealing with alcohol-related thoughts (25 min)
- Introduction to communication training (35 min)
- Identify potential upcoming high-risk situations and plan for how to cope with them (3 min)
- Assign homework (2 min)

Blood Alcohol Level Determination

Reschedule if BAL of client or partner is greater than .05. Check on compliance with homework and abstinence goal.

Overview of Session and Set Agenda (5 min)

Present today's topics and ask the couple if there are any additional issues they would like to discuss.

Review Self-Recording and Homework (5 min)

1. Collect completed self-recording cards from both the client and the partner and use the data to update the Alcohol Use and Urges and Relationship Satisfaction graphs. Reinforce the couple for compliance.

2. Review status of self-management planning. Client should select and implement two more plans for homework.

3. Review Decisional Matrix status and review negative consequences card.

4. Review alternatives to drinking; identify two more positive activities and assign.

5. Review urge discussion homework. Encourage the couple to continue to discuss urges as needed.

6. Review partner's implementation of an alternative to one of his or her behaviors that is a trigger for the client's drinking. Review the partner's completed self-management plans. Assign implementation of two more alternatives this week.

7. Review partner's completed Partner List of Protecting From Drinking worksheet. Discuss with the client and partner and add additional non-protection reactions for more difficult situations. Select one scenario for the partner to practice during the week—either in vivo or imaginal.

8. Review shared pleasurable activity together.

Check In (5 min)

Ask couple how their week was in general. Acknowledge both partners' concerns. Use information from this discussion for specific topics in the rest of the session.

If client is not abstinent at this point, discuss possible need for higher level of care.

Shared Activities Plan for Next Few Weeks (10 min)

Using the couple's completed Ideas for Enjoyable Activities worksheet from last session review the outcome of their first shared activity. Help the couple identify a shared activity for each of the next 2–3 weeks and record them on the Planning for More Enjoyable Activities worksheet in the workbook.

Dealing With Alcohol-Related Thoughts (25 min)

So far, treatment has focused on the development and rearrangement of external triggers and the development of ways to focus on negative consequences of drinking and generate positive alternatives. The emphasis in this section is on further expansion of cognitive control, teaching the client to modify what he or she says to him or herself—the rearrangement of internal or cognitive events. This will be done in two ways:

- Identifying and challenging dangerous thoughts (there are three types).

- Learning to "think through the drink"—to stop and think through the behavior chain.

Therapist Note

- *This section focuses primarily on the client's coping with his or her own thoughts and desires about drinking. The partner's involvement will be limited, but he or she should be included in the educational component to help increase understanding that dealing with negative or dysfunctional thoughts is an active rather than passive process.*

Identifying and Challenging Dangerous Thoughts

Refer the client to the section "Dealing With Thinking About Alcohol" in Chapter 7 of the workbook. Explain the 3 types of thoughts that can trigger drinking:

1. Thoughts about alcohol can create urges. Some examples include images of bars, thoughts about a favorite drink, and smells and sounds of alcohol. These thoughts directly trigger urges.

2. Thoughts about the enjoyable effects of alcohol can trigger urges. Some examples are thoughts such as "just one won't hurt"; "it will calm my nerves"; "my friends will think I'm strange if I don't drink"; "it will help me sleep"; "I can have just one." These thoughts are generally about the short-term benefits, but ignore the long-term problems.

3. Negative thinking can lead to drinking. Unpleasant thoughts and emotions can also lead to drinking. Some of these thoughts are about hopelessness or about negative self-worth. Examples are self-doubt, guilt, and anger. Negative thoughts are indirect triggers. They set up a chain of events that lead to drinking.

Alcohol-related thoughts ➔
Positive-consequence thoughts ➔ Increased probability of drinking
Negative/unpleasant thoughts ➔

Figure 10.1
Thoughts That Can Trigger Drinking

Figure 10.1 shows the three different types of thoughts that can lead to drinking.

Thinking Through the Drink

Inform the client that our thoughts and what we do in a particular situation are chained. You may use the following sample dialogue:

> *The first step to stopping the drinking chains is to recognize the thoughts. You have already listed many of your own triggers. Among these triggers you will find some dangerous thoughts. Be alert for these dangerous thoughts. When you identify a dangerous thought, challenge it, and replace it with a healthy thought.*

Exercise—Dealing With Alcohol-Related Thoughts

Have the client use the Dealing With Alcohol-Related Thoughts worksheet in the workbook to write down at least one personal example of each type of thought he or she has experienced that has led to drinking. Provide instructions as follows:

> *You feel the "urge" to drink. Write down the positive thoughts you have about alcohol when you experience this urge. Then, "think through the drink"—getting drunk, neglecting your children, upsetting your partner/family, looking awful, feeling ashamed, etc. Challenge the positive thoughts about alcohol with replacement thoughts. Now think about the reasons you don't want to drink—write these down on the bottom of the worksheet. Feel how good it is to follow through on the commitment you've made to being sober.*

Figure 10.2 shows a sample worksheet.

Therapist Note

▪ *The client should be taught procedures to modify this category of thoughts through cognitive restructuring. The rationale for these procedures should stress their use as self-control skills. Encourage a high level of client involvement in the formulation of the dangerous thoughts that may lead to drinking, as well as more healthy, replacement thoughts. Emphasize that better control of thoughts will make it easier for the client to control drinking behavior.* ▪

Dealing With Alcohol-Related Thoughts

Direct, Positive Thoughts About Alcohol:
(for example, an image of a cold glass of beer)

Beer tastes good!

Challenge and replace:

One beer tastes good. Twelve beers make me sick. I can never stop after just one so there's no point in thinking about it.

2. Thoughts About positive consequences of alcohol:
(for example, "A glass of wine will taste good")

I won't feel so lonely if I drink a lot.

Challenge and replace:

In the long run, I'll be even lonelier because I'll end up isolating those people close to me with my drinking.

3. Negative thinking:
(for example, "I'm such a loser, I might as well drink too")

I have hurt so many people. They'll never forgive me. There's no point in even trying.

Challenge and replace:

Drinking will definitely make things worse. At least I have a chance of making things right if I stay sober and am willing to try.

Figure 10.2
Example of Completed Dealing With Alcohol-Related Thoughts worksheet

Introduction to Communication Training (35 min)

The goal of this session is to begin to label some of the techniques the couple has been using to help make a transition to the sessions on formal communication skills training. In order to be clear on this, therapists should be very familiar with Chapters 4, 6, 7, and 8 of Fincham et al.'s book, *Communicating in Relationships*, and with Chapters 1, 2, 3, and 7 of Gottman et al.'s book, *A Couple's Guide to Communication*.

Therapist Note

■ *There is a lot of didactic information in this module. Your goal is to give the couple a good overview of issues related to communication and to help them learn to think deliberately about their own communication patterns. The corresponding chapter of the workbook provides more detail, and the couple can review the information during the week.* ■

Use the following sample dialogue to introduce communication training:

We have been focusing primarily on the drinking so far—both to help you (the client) *stop and to help you* (the partner) *know more about how to respond to your partner's drinking and the changes she has been making. Throughout, I've been encouraging the two of you to talk together to come up with the best strategies for you. I've been trying to help at points where you get stuck in communicating with each other. In the second half of the treatment, we're going to focus more on how the two of you communicate, and I will help you learn ways to get around the roadblocks you encounter when you're talking about difficult topics.*

Today, I want to get you started on thinking about communication. We'll be focusing on different aspects of communication each week now for the rest of the treatment. For starters, let's talk about the positive ways that you communicate.

Exercise—Positive Communication

Using the top half of the Strengths and Weaknesses in Our Communication worksheet in the workbook, have the couple list positive aspects of communication. Ask each partner what they see as positives, and then add other positive aspects of communication that you observed. Use notes and specific examples that are drawn from the individual couple's interactions to begin to label and underscore the general rules of good communication and negotiation skills.

Using the section "Keeping the Communication Lines Open" in Chapter 7 of the workbook, talk about other aspects of good communication. Be selective and highlight those aspects of positive communication that are most relevant to the couple. A copy of the information in the workbook is provided in the following page.

Keeping the Communication Lines Open

You may have begun to find it easier to talk with one another. Many little things you do add up and create a better relationship.

The way you treat each other most of the time will affect your relationship. Many people take their relationship for granted. By being pleasant most of the time, you both will handle tough times better.

The following are ways that couples can keep their lines of communication open:

Be polite. Show at least as much courtesy to your partner as you would to a stranger. Remembering such simple things as saying "please" and "thank you" show you care about your partner's feelings.

Tell your partner about the good feelings you have. Let your partner know, with words and actions, exactly what he or she does to make you feel good. Many people wrongly assume that their partner will just know these things. Expressing your feelings reminds your partner that he or she is important.

Do favors for your partner. The small things you do for one another add up. We know that couples who do many small things for one another have fewer difficulties handling disagreements. Think of it as investing in your relationship.

Stop and think before commenting on something irritating. Ask yourself if the issue is really important. Decide if the consequences of bringing up something minor are worth it.

Choose the right place and time to bring up a problem. Talk about your worries, concerns, or irritations when other things will not distract both you and your partner. Choose a time when both of you can devote your energies to the problem.

Have a goal for every complaint. Complaining for the sake of complaining does not solve much. Think of your complaint as a problem that you both should solve together. When you have a complaint, think of a specific thing that you would like changed.

If you have a complaint, stick to one thing at a time. We have a term for piling on many complaints at once. We call it "kitchen sinking." Instead of kitchen sinking, focus on one problem at a time. Bringing up many things at once will be overwhelming and may sound like blaming.

Ask for change in a positive manner. Describe what your partner can do differently and how it will make you happier. Avoid being critical.

Expect to compromise. There are two ways to compromise: (1) each of you gets a part of what you want and gives up a little of something; (2) one of you gets when you want, but in exchange, the other person may get his or her way in another situation.

At first, some of these things will be difficult. As a couple, you have developed many habits that will need to change. Often, couples get stuck because no one wants to be the first to do something positive. Remember that each of you is totally responsible for your own actions. You can do these things despite what your partner does. The benefits begin when someone (you) takes the first step.

Exercise—Negative Communication

Introduce the negative communication exercise using the following dialogue:

There are areas in which you have difficulties as well. These may be harder for you to describe—usually when couples aren't communicating well, they feel frustrated, and a natural tendency is to blame the other person ("You don't listen"). Let's see if we can describe some patterns between the two of you when communication doesn't go well. We'll be learning to change these in upcoming sessions.

Work with the couple to list negative aspects of their communication on the bottom half of the Strengths and Weaknesses in our Communication worksheet in the workbook. Ask each partner what they see as negatives, then add other aspects of negative communication you may have observed. Use notes and specific examples that are drawn from the individual couple's interactions.

Using the section "Signs of Bad Communication" in the workbook, identify other aspects of the couple's communication that are problematic. Do not go through the full list, but rather select relevant examples. A copy of the list is included here.

Signs of Bad Communication

Not listening: Listening is a complicated job. You must hear what is said, figure what was intended, check if you understand by getting feedback, and validate what the other person is saying.

Mind reading: People often assume they know what is on the other person's mind. This is a dangerous trap. The assumptions are often wrong and lead to trouble. Even if you have known someone for a long time, you can't know for sure what your partner is thinking. Always check with your partner to make sure you understand what he or she is thinking.

Yes-butting: Yes-butting is when the listener does not really listen but keeps talking about what is on his or her mind. In this bad communication, the listener will say, "Yes, but . . ." Listen and communicate to your partner that you are taking what he or she says seriously. Repeat it back to him or her in your own words.

Drifting off topic: Many couples will start an important conversation but end up talking about things not related to the main issue. By drifting around the subject, couples do not resolve important problems. When discussing a problem, stick to one issue at a time.

Interrupting: Interrupting is not only rude it also keeps the listener from ever hearing what the other person has to say. Wait until the other person finishes before speaking.

Standoff routine: Couples get into a routine of arguing and then waiting for the other person to back down. Nobody backs down because he or she would see this as losing face. Accept responsibility! Be willing to take the first steps toward making up.

Heavy silence or escalating quarrels: Two symptoms of bad communication are silent treatments and arguments that constantly get out of control. Use assertive communication skills to discuss a problem with your partner.

Never calling stop action or getting feedback: Another symptom is for couples in arguments to not stop and get feedback from each other. This communication problem means that arguments go in circles without the partners understanding one another. When arguments seem like they are going in circles, stop and ask your partner what he or she is feeling or thinking. You can then solve the misunderstandings that create bad communication.

Insulting and personally attacking each other: Insults and personal attacks just make the other person more angry. Insults make arguments worse, never better. Honey is better than vinegar when dealing with loved ones.

Not valuing what the other person says: People who put down what other people say cannot have healthy communication. Statements like "that is ridiculous" or "that is stupid" not only put down the other person they also signal poor listening. Always show respect for what your partner says.

Kitchen sinking: Kitchen sinking happens when people bring in old problems into a disagreement. The disagreement sounds like a laundry list of complaints instead of healthy problem solving. To the partner, the laundry list sounds like an attack coming from many sides. He or she will usually get defensive. Stick to one issue at a time when discussing a problem.

Character assassination: Much like insults, character assassination shows disrespect. Instead of focusing on the problem, a person talks about what is wrong with the other person. Angry partners will attack the other person instead of focusing on fixing the problem. Stick to discussing the problem.

Anticipating High-Risk Situations This Week (3 min)

Work with the client to identify at least one high-risk situation coming up in the next week (see sample dialogue in Session 1). Have the client write out ideas for handling the situation on the High-Risk Situations worksheet in the workbook. Remember to include the partner in this discussion.

Homework (2 min)

- Instruct the client to continue self-recording and record coping with high-risk situations on the back of the client self-recording cards.

- Instruct the client to continue to rehearse negative consequences from the 3 × 5 card in high-risk situations this week.

- Instruct the client to start developing new thinking habits and finish completing the Dealing With Alcohol-Related Thoughts worksheet.

- Instruct the client to implement two more stimulus-control alternative plans.

- Instruct the partner to continue recording client's alcohol use and urges (intensity), and his or her own level of relationship satisfaction using the partner recording cards.

- ✏ Remind the partner to implement two more trigger alternatives this week.
- ✏ Have the partner select and practice one non-protection scenario during the week.
- ✏ Ask the couple to carry out one shared pleasurable activity together.
- ✏ Have the couple read Chapter 7 of the workbook.

Chapter 11 — Session 8: Drink Refusal / Communication Part II

(Corresponds to chapter 8 of the workbook)

Materials Needed

- Copy of the couple's workbook
- Breathalyzer and 2 tubes
- Partner and client self-recording cards
- Alcohol Use and Urges and Relationship Satisfaction graphs in progress
- Extending the Shared Activity worksheet
- High-Risk Situations worksheet

Outline

- Determine blood alcohol level (BAL) of both the client and his or her partner
- Provide overview of session (5 min)
- Review self-recording and homework (10 min)
- Check in (5 min)
- Work with the couple to refine and extend their shared activity (10 min)
- Teach client how to refuse a drink (25 min)
- Introduce the model of good communication (25 min)

- Identify potential upcoming high-risk situations and plan for how to cope with them (5 min)
- Assign homework (5 min)

Blood Alcohol Level Determination

Reschedule if BAL of client or partner is greater than .05. Check on compliance with homework and abstinence goal.

Overview of Session and Set Agenda (5 min)

Inform couple of topics that will be covered in the session. Ask the couple if there are any additional issues they would like to discuss today.

Review Self-Recording and Homework (10 min)

1. Review self-recording, update graphs, and reinforce client.
2. Review use of 3 × 5 card in high-risk situations.
3. Review application of all past exercises and self-management plans; Problems? Questions? Determine if any new situations have occurred requiring a plan; reinforce increased self-control, new thinking patterns, rehearsal.
4. Review Dealing With Alcohol-Related Thoughts homework.
5. Review partner's implementation of more trigger alternatives.
6. Review partner's practice of a non-protection scenario during the week.
7. Review shared pleasurable activity for the week.

Check In (5 min)

Ask couple how their week was in general. Acknowledge both partners' concerns. Use information from this for specific topics in the rest of the session.

Extending the Shared Activity (10 min)

Using the Extending the Shared Activity worksheet in the workbook, help the couple refine the shared activity by asking each partner to list three behaviors that they would like to see increased in each other during the fun activity (e.g., if couple agrees to go out to dinner, client may want partner to offer to hang up his or her coat, or to hold hands, or give him or her a compliment). Explain that the overall intent is to increase the positive experiences they have with each other. Also note that any changes that one partner requests should be acceptable to the other partner, but that they are agreeing to do these to make the other person happy. Ensure that the items are simple and not too demanding. Encourage the couple to make positive constructive requests rather than complaints (e.g., she *never* holds my hand anymore). Once lists are refined, have the couple share their lists and agree to implement these requests during the planned pleasurable activity. Assign another shared activity this week.

Drink Refusal Training (25 min)

Therapist Note

■ *The drink refusal training this week focuses specifically on helping the client to develop effective refusal skills. Next week's session will address the role of the partner. Tell the couple that this is the sequence of training, emphasizing the importance of the client having his or her own skills and ability to deal with drinking situations, whether or not the partner is available.* ■

Inform the client that the ability to refuse drinks is a special case of assertiveness, however, one-third of alcoholic patients relapse as a direct result of social pressure from "friends" to drink.

The ability to refuse drinks is much more difficult than it appears. It is another weapon in your arsenal of self-control skills. We are going to practice ways of refusing/turning down drinks so that you can gain control in these tough situations.

Expect resistance during this exercise. The client may say, "Refusing drinks is not a problem," to which you can reply, *"Yes, but it's a good skill to have anyway."*

Exercise—How to Refuse a Drink

Introduce the drink refusal exercise using the following dialogue:

Use this rule of thumb: Remember that individuals who offer you drinks are "pushers" and must be discouraged politely but firmly.

Refusing offers of drinks is harder than most people think. It takes special skills to say no to drinks.

Offers of drinks come in many forms. Sometimes friends or co-workers put pressure on you to join in their drinking. Other times the pressure comes from family members. Sometimes you may be concerned about what others will think if you refuse a drink.

Some people are easier to refuse than others. Some will politely accept your first refusal. Others may get pushy.

Drink refusal is an important assertiveness skill. The foundation of assertiveness skills is a respect for your own needs. Be firm without getting aggressive. By using the following skills, you can refuse a drink without coming on too strong.

"No" should be the first thing you say. Starting with "no" makes it tougher for the pusher to try to manipulate you.

Look the person in the eye when you speak. Eye contact makes you come across as firm. Not looking the other person in the eye tells her that you are not sure about what you are saying.

Speak clearly and in a serious tone. Your manner should say that you mean business.

You have a right to say no. You want to stay sober. It is your life that you are protecting. Do not feel guilty.

Suggest alternatives. If someone is offering a drink, ask for something non-alcoholic. If someone is asking you to get into a risky situation, suggest something else that is not risky.

Change the subject to a new topic of conversation. Get the pusher to think about something else.

Ask the person not to continue offering you a drink. Someone who is pushing you to drink is not respecting your rights. Ask her to leave you alone.

Know your bottom line. You are saying no out of respect for yourself. If the person keeps pushing, use your problem-solving skills. Remember, you can leave, get the person to leave, or you can get help from others.

And finally, remember to practice, practice, practice!

Drink Refusal Case Examples

Refer the client to the drink refusal examples in the workbook and go over them as follows:

You're at your brother's house on Christmas Day. It's a special occasion: you're with family and friends. He says, "How about a beer?" You say, "No thanks, I'd like a Coke, though."

A group of your friends stop by your house or approach you at a party and offer you a drink. They say, "Hey Jill, how about a glass of wine?" You say, "No thanks, I'm not drinking." They say, "Oh come on, one drink won't hurt you. What kind of friend are you?" or "What's the matter? Are you too good to drink with us?" You say, *"I'll just take a mineral water with lime, thanks."*

Exercise—Role-Play

Construct at least three typical scenes in which the client has had difficulty refusing a drink or has been encouraged to drink (use functional analysis and DPQ for examples).

Now pick an example from the client's life and practice drink-refusal role-play in session. You will play the part of the client while the client plays the part of the pusher. Then, you will switch roles.

Therapist Note

■ *Most clients will have trouble just saying no. A good procedure is to teach the components of refusal one at a time (i.e., have the client say no, then practice changing the topic). After each role-play, have the client evaluate the effectiveness of his or her response. Role reversal where the client plays the part of the pusher and you play the part of the client saying no is a helpful technique. In addition, the client should be asked to refuse three separate times in each scene.* ■

Communication Skills (25 min)

Using the information on good communication in the workbook, introduce the model of good communication (sender, message, filter, receiver) that describes the events that intervene between the speaker's intended message and its impact or how the listener hears it. A copy of the information from the workbook is provided for your use on the following page.

Good Communication

Many disagreements start when one person misunderstands what the other person is saying. Many things can happen to create misunderstandings. Communication is a very complicated thing that we take for granted. One partner may wish to say something. We call this the *intent*. The other partner may understand something completely different from what the first partner wished to say. This is called the *impact* of the statement. Many things get between the intent and the impact of a message. Some of these things are called filters. Filters change a message to be something different from what the speaker intended. Both the speaker and the listener have filters that change a message.

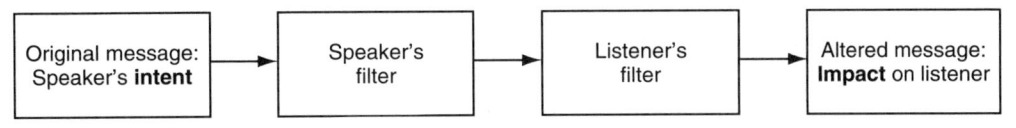

Original message: Speaker's **intent** → Speaker's filter → Listener's filter → Altered message: **Impact** on listener

The speaker intends to say something, but the listener hears something else. Notice what happens in the following situation:

John has had a hard day at work. He was up against a deadline, and his boss was in his office and emailing him every half hour. He's very tired, but he and Rachel are going out to dinner with a woman Rachel knew from high school, and her husband. Rachel is very tense about the dinner—she wants to look good because this woman was very popular and pretty and Rachel had felt a little inferior to her when they were in high school. John is tired and distracted and is still worrying that he might have overlooked something in the project, but doesn't say anything to Rachel because he doesn't want to ruin the evening by focusing on work.

Rachel (Wanting reassurance that she looks good):   Do these pants look okay on me?

John (Always thinks she looks great and doesn't realize that she's insecure, is still worrying about work):   Yeah, they're fine.

Rachel (Thinks he's saying she looks bad):   Do you think I should change?

John (Still distracted):   No, you're fine.

Rachel (Now she is convinced that she looks terrible and that he's half-ignoring her because he doesn't want to go out):   Look, I don't care if you don't want to go out; this is important to me. I want to look good, and I want you to be on your best behavior too.

John (Totally confused that she's upset):   I don't understand why you're so worked up about this—it's only dinner with an old friend, and you look good—you always look good.

Rachel (Angry):   Don't patronize me. I hate it when you do that!

Notice that John's intent was to compliment Rachel, but because of his own distraction and bad mood, he didn't sound complimentary. Rachel didn't know he was upset, so she tried to guess what he was thinking. She guessed wrong but never realized it.

continued

Good Communication *continued*

Good communication means having the impact you intended to have. That is, intent equals impact. Good communication between partners is clear and specific. The speaker tries to clarify the intent of his or her message by stating exactly what he or she is thinking, wanting, or feeling. He or she does not assume the listener can mind-read. The good listener tries to make sure that he or she understands the intent of the message. He or she does not try to guess at meanings.

Misunderstandings often happen. Sometimes they lead to funny stories. Other times they poison the relationship. You will have a better relationship if you understand that communication can be very complicated. There are many ways for things to go wrong. In John and Rachel's example, they were tired and nervous about the evening. Their emotional and physical condition affected how they heard each other. They probably have some history of misunderstandings that contributed to this problem. Both John and Rachel had filters that affected their communication. Filters change a message from what they intend to what they hear. The following are some examples of filters that affect the speaker and the listener. Notice that the filters are similar for both of them.

Speaker filters	Listener filters
Not saying what we really mean. In the example, the speakers were not clear in speaking what was on their mind.	**Often we do not listen because we are thinking about a response.** Not paying attention leads to the person ignoring everything the speaker says.
Leaving out information or assuming the listener already knows something. We often expect the listener to know why we are saying something. The problem is that listeners are not mind readers.	**Making assumptions based on too little information.** The listeners in our story assumed that there were hidden reasons behind what the speaker said.
Moods often affect the way we say something. In this example, Rachel might have said things differently if she had not been so tense. Moods affect how we say things.	**Moods affect how we interpret what someone else says.** If we are in a happy mood, we will hear something as funny. If we are tired and worried, we may hear the same words as threatening.
The history of problems in the relationship may affect our communication. If things our partner has done irritate us, we will not put the same care into saying something. Many couples bring unrelated problems into a disagreement.	**The history of problems in the relationship** may affect how we hear what our partner says. Old problems influence how we interpret what the other person is saying. We may suspect they connect the current statement to the old problem.

Ask the couple if they have had the experience of being misunderstood by their partner.

If the two of you are talking and feeling misheard or misunderstood, you want to figure out what is going wrong. The best way to do that is to get feedback from your partner. Only when you know what your partner thought you meant can you figure out where the discussion went off track. Most couples don't do this—they assume they know exactly what their partner meant and end up angry, hurt, or sad.

A constructive way to get feedback is to use the "check-out and paraphrase" method (Gottman et al., 1976, p.16). This skill involves several steps:

1. *Call a stop action: You stop the discussion so you can talk about it.*

2. *Feedback: Ask for feedback—what did your partner think you said? If you are asked for feedback, be brief and to the point. Keep in mind that you are trying to sort through a misunderstanding, not making points to win.*

3. *Listen to feedback: What does your partner think you said? How is your partner feeling right now? What is the content? What is the feeling?*

4. *Summarize and validate: Summarize the content of what was said and your partner's feelings. Try to look at it from your partner's point of view to understand why your partner feels this way. Communicate your understanding of your partner's feelings—if you were seeing things his way, it would make sense to feel that way. Saying you understand your partner's feelings does not mean you agree, only that you are listening and trying to understand. This is very hard to do, especially when you yourself feel hurt or not listened to.*

5. *Check impact. Think about your partner's reaction compared to your original intent. If there's a gap between what you meant ("intent") and how it hit your partner ("impact"), try to clarify your meaning.*

Ask the couple for their reactions and if they have any questions about the model.

Exercise—Check-Out and Paraphrase

Once the model is understood, choose an example from the couple's expressed problems that is relatively low in conflict and emotional content. Then have the couple role play the essential first steps in improving communication, following the 5 steps just described.

For homework, ask the couple to have a discussion during the week on an issue in which they have *mild* conflict. Emphasize that they should not try to solve any problem, just study what they do when they try to communicate. In doing this homework, introduce couple to the idea of scheduling a "couple meeting"—at a formal time, set aside a specific period of time (15 min, maximum) to do nothing else but talk about one topic.

Anticipating High-Risk Situations This Week (5 min)

Work with the client to identify at least one high-risk situation coming up in the next week (see sample dialogue in Session 1). Have the client write out ideas for handling the situation on the High-Risk Situations worksheet in the workbook. Remember to include the partner in this discussion.

Homework (5 min)

- Instruct the client to continue self-recording and record coping with high-risk situations on the back of the client self-recording cards.
- Determine a situation during the next week in which the client will be offered alcohol. Contract with the client to practice refusal scenes twice daily.
- Instruct the client to continue employing self-control procedures.
- Instruct the partner to continue recording client's alcohol use and urges (intensity), and his or her own level of relationship satisfaction using the partner recording cards in the workbook.

- ✎ Have the couple participate in a shared activity with three requested new behaviors for each partner.

- ✎ Instruct the couple to have a discussion on a topic around which they have mild disagreement and to practice the 5-step good communication technique practiced in the session.

- ✎ Have the couple read Chapter 8 of the workbook.

Chapter 12

Session 9: Partner Role in Drink Refusal / Communication Part III / Relapse Prevention Part I

(Corresponds to chapter 9 of the workbook)

Materials Needed

- Copy of couple's workbook
- Breathalyzer and 2 tubes
- Partner and client self-recording cards
- Alcohol Use and Urges and Relationship Satisfaction graphs in progress
- When Alcohol is Present worksheet
- X, Y, Z Worksheet
- Seemingly Irrelevant Decisions worksheet
- High-Risk Situations worksheet

Outline

- Determine blood alcohol level (BAL) of both the client and his or her partner
- Provide overview of session (5 min)
- Review self-recording and homework (5 min)
- Check in (5 min)
- Discuss the partner's role in drink situations and how he or she can help the client refuse drinks (15 min)

189

- Teach the couple how to use leveling and editing to foster good communication (15 min)

- Introduce the concept of "seemingly irrelevant decisions" and how certain actions that may have nothing to do with drinking can lead the client to drink (35 min)

- Identify potential upcoming high-risk situations and plan for how to cope with them (5 min)

- Assign homework (5 min)

Blood Alcohol Level Determination

Reschedule if BAL of client or partner is greater than .05. Check on compliance with homework and abstinence goal.

Overview of Session and Set Agenda (5 min)

Inform couple of topics that will be covered in the session. Ask the couple if there are any additional issues they would like to discuss today.

Review Self-Recording and Homework (5 min)

1. Review self-recording, update graphs, and reinforce couple for recording behavior. Ask about past homework reviews, "spontaneous" rewards, covert rehearsal, etc.

2. Review week regarding problem situations encountered and application of self-control procedures.

3. Review drink refusal training homework assignment. Problems? Questions?

4. Review shared activity homework.

5. Review use of 5-step communication model. For homework, have the couple practice discussing another problem, using the stop action again. Suggest that when the couple calls a "stop action" in

any problematic interaction, each partner should ask themselves the following questions:

- Where was I pig-headed?
- Where was I not listening?
- What was my partner trying to say?
- What was my partner feeling?

Again emphasize that we are simply teaching the couple to identify and analyze their own communication. They should not try to solve problems completely or get into arguments over these exercises.

Check In (5 min)

Ask couple how their week was in general. Acknowledge both partners' concerns. Use information from this for specific topics in the rest of the session.

Partner Role in Drink Situations and in Drink Refusal (15 min)

During this part of the session, the partner may have some questions including, "Should I not drink in front of my abstinent partner?" or "Should I serve drinks if guests come by now that my partner is abstinent?" or "What do I do when we're out together and drinks are being served?" Ask the couple whether any of these questions has come up and open a discussion on the topic. Emphasize that there are no "right" answers, just ones that work well for them. Be careful to deal constructively with difficult client–partner interactions. Suggest to the couple that they could try to discuss approaches to situations *before* they happen.

It is helpful to remind clients that avoiding drinking is the responsibility of the problem drinker. There will always be tempting drinking situations and the partner cannot be at each one anyway. Drinking or not drinking is a personal choice made over and over again by the person with the drinking problem alone, and it will have to be made in many daily situations. You may use the following information from the workbook to facilitate discussion.

For the Partner—How Can I Help When Alcohol Is Present

As a couple, you may be together in many situations where alcohol is present. When this happens, it is important to remember the following:

- It is the drinker's responsibility to decide not to drink, but as the partner, you can help.
- You may make it easier for your partner to stay sober and you'll feel better knowing what you can do to help.
- The key is to talk ahead of time about what you can do.

Here's an example. Leonard and Suzanne had some friends over for dinner. Leonard usually is generous with drinks, but didn't offer them any alcohol:

Suzanne: You usually give Harold and Maude drinks, why didn't you tonight?

Leonard: Because I was helping you stay sober.

Suzanne: Well that makes me mad because I feel like a baby. Why should others be deprived because of me? I felt so embarrassed!

Leonard: Well I was only helping since you've been off it such a short time.

Suzanne: You are patronizing me. I am getting mad.

Leonard: No I am not; I am helping you, dear!

Suzanne: Well that kind of help I don't need! You don't understand me at all!

Leonard thought he was helping, but without talking to Suzanne first, he made the situation worse. He could have asked Suzanne ahead of time:

Leonard: Harold and Maude are coming over tonight. I usually offer them drinks before dinner. I wonder what you think would be most helpful for you tonight.

Suzanne: I don't want them to feel deprived. Seeing them drink won't give me an urge.

Suzanne also could have looked ahead and talked with Leonard:

Suzanne: Harold and Maude are coming over tonight. It's okay with me if you serve them drinks, but don't ask me what I want—just give me a seltzer with a twist, and don't say anything about my not drinking. I'm not ready to tell them yet.

There are lots of ways to help:

- Offer to get your partner a non-alcoholic drink so she doesn't have to go to the bar.
- Order the non-alcoholic drink of your partner's choice in a restaurant, or say nothing so that your partner can order herself.

continued

For the Partner—How Can I Help When Alcohol Is Present *continued*

- Give your partner a warm look, or touch your partner for a moment to let her know you're thinking about him or her in a drinking situation.

- Be willing to leave a social event early if your partner's just having too hard a time.

- Join the conversation if you think someone is pushing your partner too hard and she is getting frustrated.

- Keep in mind that your partner hasn't been sober that long and that any situation with alcohol present may be a challenge.

Remember—there are no right answers—just be sure that you know how your partner wants you to help.

Exercise—Drink Refusal Situations

Using the When Alcohol is Present worksheet in the workbook, guide the couple to a discussion of what the partner can do to help the problem drinker in typical drink-refusal situations, but *not* by taking decision-making control or responsibility away. Discuss some typical situations where the couple would be together and alcohol would be present. Generate actions for the partner that are acceptable to the couple and record them on the worksheet. Make sure the couple agrees on the behaviors so that there are no mixed messages (e.g., a hand squeeze could mean, "Watch it, I don't trust you"). Choose one situation, have the couple record it on the worksheet, and use it to conduct a role-play in session. Ask the couple to discuss for homework two other high-risk drinking situations and how they might handle alternatives together and practice in one situation if possible. Make sure the partner *does not take control over the situation* from the problem drinker too early, thus protecting her from being assertive and taking away personal responsibility.

Communication Skills: Leveling and Editing (15 min)

Use this session to build on the previous two sessions and to focus on one or two examples chosen from the couple's problems. Paraphrase the following after making sure the couple understands the basic principles of good and bad communication. (Review pages 27-60 in Gottman's book for this session.)

> *In this session, we will explore direct and assertive communication. Couples usually have distinct patterns of communication:*
>
> - *Some couples mostly have dull, boring non-communication when there are lots of things under the surface that are being avoided.*
>
> - *Some couples are the opposite—quarreling and bickering are frequent and usually escalate.*
>
> *Arguing or fighting is the most obvious pattern of conflict in relationships. Research shows that people are more polite to strangers than to their partners. Many couples get themselves into a pattern of*

saying anything they may be thinking. They do not stop to consider whether it is insulting or senseless. They interrupt their partners more, put their partners down more, hurt each other's feelings more, and are less complimentary to each other.

For this type of fighting, the partners need more politeness and editing. To break this pattern, the individuals need to stop and think about the importance and damage caused by what they will say. Everyone must learn how to edit out unimportant or insulting things that will poison communication. Partners must realize that they cannot say everything that is on their mind. As previously discussed, our thoughts are not always healthy.

The second pattern of couple conflict is avoidance. Avoidance happens when one partner gives in most of the time, or both partners quietly ignore a problem issue. Although the couple never seems to disagree, they are in conflict as someone usually feels resentful or unappreciated. Some issues are important and need to be discussed.

The way to break out of both patterns is to:

- *Become more aware of your own feelings—what makes you feel good and what makes you feel unhappy.*
- *Level with your partner about what he or she does that makes you unhappy. Tell your partner what he or she can do to change the situation. A constructive way to level is to use statements like the following: "I feel X, when you do Y, in situation Z."*

Ask the couple if they think one pattern of communication or the other is more like them. Ask for examples.

Of course, many couples go back and forth—sometimes they say too much, other times they sit on their feelings and don't express them.

The same solution works for both kinds of couples—learning how to express thoughts and feelings assertively. For couples who avoid conflict, learning to be assertive means learning to "level" more about your feelings. For couples who argue a lot, learning to be assertive means learning to "edit" your feelings more carefully and being less aggressive.

"Leveling" means being clear with your partner about what you are feeling without being cruel. "Editing" means being more polite to each other—thinking about the other person's feelings and treating them with common courtesy when you express your feelings about something.

For most of us, it is difficult to do a good job at leveling or editing because it is easy to slip into saying what the other person is doing wrong, rather than saying what you are feeling. It is also important to realize that each partner must learn how to receive feedback. A good receiver responds by paraphrasing and validating what the speaker is saying, and tries not to be defensive or to attack.

Focus explicitly on an example from the couple's interaction. You will also get a chance to re-emphasize constructive and destructive communications that were covered in previous sessions. Also focus on the importance of choosing the right time, place, and moods before deciding to level.

Introduce the X, Y, Z statements as a way to integrate being more assertive, expressing feelings, and avoiding destructive ways of leveling (see Gottman et al., p. 38).

Using the section "Handling Relationship Conflict" in Chapter 9 of the workbook, explain constructive ways of leveling.

A constructive way to level is to use statements like the following: "I feel X, when you do Y, in situation Z."

You have to be as specific as you can about X, Y, and Z. Examples of constructive leveling are:

1. *"I feel stressed and hassled when you ask me for things when we first get up in the morning."*
2. *"I feel lonely and embarrassed when you don't introduce me to people at a party and don't spend time with me."*
3. *"I feel hurt when you criticize my driving."*
4. *"I feel angry when you spend money that is not in our budget." All of these statements are assertive, and they specify the* **feeling** *(X), the* **action** *(Y), and the* **situation** *(Z).*

Exercise—Using X, Y, Z Statements

Using the X, Y, Z, Worksheet in the workbook, have the couple develop some X, Y, Z statements for five simple issues and write them down on the worksheet. A sample worksheet is shown in Figure 12.1.

X, Y, Z Worksheet

1. I feel worried when you get home late from work.

2. I feel hurt when you don't come to the phone when I call you at work.

3. I feel left out when you and your daughter talk about "girly" things for a long time when we're all together at dinner.

4. I feel angry when you won't tell me what's wrong when you're obviously upset.

5. I feel frustrated and angry when you forget to balance the checkbook and then a check bounces.

Figure 12.1
Example of Completed X, Y, Z, Worksheet

Seemingly Irrelevant Decisions (35 min)

Therapist Note

■ *Both partners may be involved in making seemingly irrelevant decisions, either together or independently. Involve both of them in the discussion, but focus more on the client's decision making. Either partner, however, may provide examples of a seemingly irrelevant decision that resulted in drinking.* ■

Present the following rationale to the client:

> Many of the ordinary, mundane choices that are made every day seem to have nothing at all to do with drinking. Although they may not

involve making a direct choice of whether to drink, they may move you, one small step at a time, closer to being confronted with that choice. Through a series of minor decisions, you may gradually work your way closer to the point at which drinking becomes very likely. These seemingly unimportant decisions that may in fact put you on the road to drinking are called "seemingly irrelevant decisions."

To illustrate this process, consider the following story about a drinker explaining her most recent relapse—where are the seemingly irrelevant decisions?

Exercise—Seemingly Irrelevant Decisions

Present the following story to the couple and have them follow along using the Seemingly Irrelevant Decisions worksheet in the workbook:

Jeff is on his way home from work and hasn't had a drink in 5 months. He's gotten to the point where he catches himself not thinking about alcohol for 2 to 3 days at a time. It's hot outside and he wants to get home, but today there's a 10 million dollar lottery and he wants to stop to buy a couple of lottery tickets on the way home. He pulls into the liquor store/bar he used to frequent; he knows they sell lottery tickets there. He buys the tickets and is about to turn around and walk out when he hears his name being called. He looks behind him and sees Rich, an old drinking buddy, waving him over to the bar. He walks over to say hi and finds an ice-cold beer that Rich has ordered for him, waiting at the counter. Before he can stop himself, he downs the beer and orders another.

Process the story with the couple using the following sample dialogue:

Now that you've heard the story, you may be able to see that Jeff made a series of decisions that led up to his final decision to drink some beer. In your workbook, underline each one of the choice points where Jeff could have made a different decision that would have taken him away from a dangerous situation. (Did he really have to stop at a liquor store? Couldn't he have gone to a convenience store? Did he have to walk over to his old drinking buddy, or could he have waved hello to him?)

So you can see that Jeff made a series of decisions, each of which contributed in some way to his finally having some beer.

People often think of themselves as victims: "Things just seemed to happen in such a way that I ended up in a situation and then had a drink—I couldn't help it." They don't recognize how perhaps dozens of their "little" decisions, over a period of time, gradually brought them closer and closer to their predicament. It's easier to play "Monday morning quarterback" with these decisions than to recognize them when you are actually in the midst of the decision-making process. That is because so many choices don't actually seem to involve drinking at the time. Each choice you make may only take you just a little bit closer to having to make that big choice. But when alcohol isn't on your mind, it's hard to make the connection between drinking and a minor decision that seems very far removed from drinking.

The best solution is to think about every choice you have to make, no matter how seemingly irrelevant it is to drinking. By thinking ahead about each possible option you have and where each of them may lead, you can anticipate dangers that may lie along certain paths. It may feel awkward at first to have to consider everything so carefully, but after awhile, it becomes second nature and happens automatically, without much effort.

By paying more attention to the decision-making process, you'll have a greater chance to interrupt the chain of decisions that could lead to a relapse. This is important because it's much easier to stop the process early, before you wind up in a high-risk situation, than later, when you're in a situation that's harder to handle and you may be exposed to a number of triggers.

Also, by paying attention to your decision-making process, you'll be able to recognize certain kinds of thoughts that can lead to making risky decisions, such as the thought Jeff had that he "had to stop" at a bar for lottery tickets in the example above. Thoughts like "I have to" go to a party, "have to" see a certain drinking friend, or "have to" drive by a particular place often occur at the beginning of a "seemingly irrelevant decision" and should be treated as a warning or "red flag." Other "red flag" thoughts often start with "It doesn't matter if I . . ." or "I can handle . . ."

When faced with a decision, you should generally choose a low-risk option, to avoid putting yourself in a risky situation. On the other hand, you may for some reason decide to select a high-risk option. If you make this choice, you must also plan how to protect yourself while in the high-risk situation. It is usually much easier to decide to avoid a high-risk situation before you get too close to it than it is to resist temptation once you are in it.

Exercise—Discussion

Ask the client to think about the most recent time he or she drank. Help the client trace back through the decision-making chain. What was the starting point? (Exposure to a trigger? Certain thoughts?) Can the client recognize the choice points where he or she chose to make a risky decision?

Ask the client to suggest a low-risk option for the following "seemingly irrelevant decisions" situations:

- whether to keep liquor in the house
- whether to offer an ex-drinking friend a ride home
- whether to go to a bar to see old drinking friends
- where to go to get a snack/cigarettes
- whether to tell a friend that you have quit drinking or keep it a secret
- what route to take when driving (i.e., to go past or take a detour to avoid a favorite bar, liquor store, etc.)

For homework, have the client think about a decision he or she has made recently or is about to make. The decision could involve any aspect of the client's life, such as his or her job, recreational activities, friends, or family. Identify safe choices and choices that might increase the client's risk for relapse. Have the client complete the Seemingly Irrelevant Decisions worksheet.

Anticipating High-Risk Situations This Week (5 min)

Work with the client to identify at least one high-risk situation coming up in the next week (see sample dialogue in Session 1). Have the client write out ideas for handling the situation on the High-Risk Situations worksheet in the workbook. Remember to include the partner in this discussion.

Homework (5 min)

- Instruct client to continue self-recording and record coping with high-risk situations on the back of the client self-recording cards.

- Have the client complete the Seemingly Irrelevant Decisions worksheet in the workbook using a decision he or she had made recently or is about to make.

- Instruct the partner to continue recording the client's alcohol use and urges (intensity), and his or her own level of relationship satisfaction using the partner recording cards in the workbook.

- Have the couple decide together how to handle two more drink refusal situations.

- Instruct the couple to role-play at home or practice in a real situation the partner's role in drink refusal.

- Ask the couple to discuss another topic at home, selecting one at a moderate level of disagreement, using the "good communication" skills learned before, and incorporating X, Y, Z feedback as needed.

- Have the couple read Chapter 9 of the workbook.

Chapter 13 — Session 10: Problem Solving / Relapse Prevention Part II

(Corresponds to chapter 10 of the workbook)

Materials Needed

- Copy of couple's workbook
- Breathalyzer and 2 tubes
- Partner and client self-recording cards
- Alcohol Use and Urges and Relationship Satisfaction graphs in progress
- Problem-Solving Worksheet
- Family Meeting Worksheet
- Identifying and Managing Relapse Warning Signs worksheet
- High-Risk Situations worksheet

Outline

- Determine blood alcohol level (BAL) of both the client and his or her partner
- Provide overview of session (5 min)
- Review self-recording and homework (5 min)
- Check in (5 min)
- Teach the couple how to problem solve and use it as a general coping skill (20 min)
- Introduce the couple to joint problem solving (25 min)

- Discuss ways of identifying and managing warning signs of relapse (including partner role) (20 min)
- Identify potential upcoming high-risk situations and plan for how to cope with them (5 min)
- Assign homework (5 min)

Blood Alcohol Level Determination

Reschedule if BAL of client or partner is greater than .05. Check on compliance with homework and abstinence goal.

Overview of Session and Set Agenda (5 min)

Inform couple of topics that will be covered in the session. Ask the couple if there are any additional issues they would like to discuss today.

Review Self-Recording and Homework (5 min)

1. Review self-recording (drinking, urges), update graphs, provide feedback and reinforcement to both the client and the partner.
2. Review skills covered thus far, including self-management, rehearsal of negatives of drinking, drink refusal, etc.
3. Review completed Seemingly Irrelevant Decisions worksheet.
4. Review homework on partner role in drink refusal.
5. Review couple's practice of good communication skills.

Check In (5 min)

Ask couple how their week was in general. Acknowledge both partners' concerns. Use information from this for specific topics in the rest of the session.

Problem Solving as a General Coping Skill (20 min)

Point out to the client that problem-solving skills are a very important part of changing behavior and learning to negotiate changes:

We will focus in this session on using problem solving as a general coping skill. First, I'll describe what problem solving is and how to do it. Then, we'll apply problem solving to an individual problem that you (the client) *are concerned about. Finally, we'll apply the same problem-solving approach to a problem that you as a couple have been concerned about.*

Exercise—Problem Solving

Emphasis should be placed on training problem-solving *techniques*, rather than only trying to solve a specific problem, in order to increase generalization. Review the general outline of problem-solving procedures. Problem solving consists of seven steps (tell the couple to follow along using the workbook).

1. Gather information: Think about the problem situation. Who is involved? When does it happen? Exactly what takes place? What effect does this have on you? What happens before the problem (the antecedents)? What keeps the problem going (the consequences)? Where does it occur? How does the problem affect you?

2. Define the problem: What is the goal that you would like to achieve? Be clear and specific. Many people get into trouble at this step because they select very vague goals. Define your goal as something that can be counted. The more specific and real you make the problem, the easier it will be to solve.

3. Brainstorm for alternatives: This can be a fun step. The goal of this step is to build a long list of possible solutions. The first rule of brainstorming is that no idea is too silly or dumb. Try to think about any and every possible solution to the problem. Do not think about how good or bad each idea is—that will come later. By not evaluating the ideas as they come, you will be

more creative in thinking of solutions. Make as long a list as you can. The number of ideas is more important than their quality.

4. Now, consider the consequences of each: For each of your alternatives, list the positive and negative consequences. Think about the short-term and long-term results of each solution. Ask yourself: What things can you reasonably expect to happen? What will be the positive consequences? What will be the negative consequences? Which consequences will happen right away? Which consequences will happen later? How can you combine different alternatives?

5. Decide: Which of the alternatives is the most likely to achieve the goal you set in Step 2? Look for the solution (or solutions) that have the best balance of consequences.

6. Do it! The best plan in the world is useless if you do not put it into action. Try it out.

7. Evaluate: Check out how the plan is working. Which parts work best? Which parts can you improve? Fix what can be fixed.

Explain to the couple that problem-solving techniques can also be applied to almost any problematic situation in their lives. Together, choose a problem that has come up over the sessions for the client.

1. Ask the client to imagine that the situation is occurring and have him or her describe how he or she views or defines the problem. Help the client conceptualize the essence of the problem.

2. Ask the client to generate alternative ways of responding to the situation (e.g., one alternative would be the typical response the client would have to the situation) once the situation has been defined. Remember brainstorming for alternatives means don't evaluate too soon, let your mind go and the more ideas the merrier.

3. Determine with the client the full range of consequences that would result from each proposed alternative. (i.e., positive and negative, both long and short term).

4. Help the client select the most viable alternative (highest probability of gaining desired result).

5. Have the client make a commitment to implementing a solution.

6. Have the client generate alternatives for each target situation and arrive at a solution.

7. Have client commit to trying the solution and agree to evaluate how it went.

Review the sample Problem-Solving Worksheet shown in Figure 13.1 and use the blank worksheet in the workbook to practice problem solving with the client in session. Pick a problem that has come up in the course of treatment so far.

Joint Problem Solving (25 min)

Therapist Note

■ *Review Gottman et al. (1976), pp. 61–69, which provides the framework for this part of the session* ■

Introduce joint problem solving using the following dialogue:

> *Now let's talk about how problem solving can work for the two of you. It's important that you set aside time each week to talk about issues and concerns. Having a set "family meeting" time can make it easier to deal with problems. And, it's important to use all the good communication skills we've been focusing on for the past few sessions when you have a family meeting.*

Suggest that family meetings be scheduled 1–2 times per week to talk about conflicts in the relationship and how to resolve them.

> *Constant complaining without solutions is a sign of bad communication. Gripes are complaints about small or less important irritations that create conflict. You should not bring up every gripe since this may lead to bickering. One way to talk about these gripes in a healthy way is the family meeting. The family meeting is an opportunity for you and other family members to come together to solve problems. The family meeting is a special time for working on the things that create conflict. Family meetings can be scheduled 1 or 2*

Problem-Solving Worksheet

Pick a problem that has come up in the course of treatment so far and practice solving it using the methods just described.

1. Gather Information: <u>Sometimes my partner won't talk to me and I think she's angry at me. That's when we have our worst fights.</u>

2. Problem Definition: <u>I overreact when my partner won't talk to me.</u>

3. Brainstorming for Solutions and Listing of Pros and Cons:

Solution	Pros (short and long term)	Cons (short and long term)
a. Ask my partner what's wrong.	Gives her a chance to tell me. Keeps things calm	It's hard to stay calm
b. Ask my partner if she's upset with me	Same as above	I may not want to hear what has to say.
c. Take a deep breath and go for a walk if my partner says she doesn't want to talk to me.	Avoids confrontation. Gives me a chance to calm down	It's hard to walk away sometimes
d. Remind myself that my partner has other problems in her life	It's the truth. Makes me feel sympathetic instead of angry	N/A
e. Get into an argument	I can vent and blow off steam	I may hurt my partner's feelings and make things worse

4. Pick solution(s): <u>a, b, c, and d</u>

5. Implement the solution for a period of time.

6. Reevaluate the solution—Did it work? <u>Solution C seemed to work the best.</u>
If not, do problem solving again

Figure 13.1

Example of Completed Problem-Solving Worksheet

times a week at a specific time. It is a time to use good communication skills. A family meeting has three stages:

1. *Gripe time*
2. *Agenda building*
3. *Problem solving*

Stage 1—Gripe Time

Gripe time is an opportunity to express feelings and concerns. Encourage both partners to use X, Y, Z feedback during this time. Tell the couple:

Each of you should have an opportunity to state your gripes. It doesn't mean that you agree or disagree with the gripes. It's just a chance to get things out on the table. It is a time to use listening skills and empathy (put yourself in your partner's shoes). Also, you should follow the list of do's and don'ts in the workbook.

Do's and Don'ts are shown in Table 13.1.

Stage 2—Agenda Building

During this phase of the meeting, the couple has to decide what issues they want to resolve out of all the gripes and problems that have been brought up. It is best to limit the discussion to one major topic in a session. Features of good and bad problem definitions are provided for the couple in the workbook and shown here in Table 13.2.

Table 13.1 Do's and Don'ts of Problem Solving

Do's	Don'ts
State your gripes clearly and specifically	**Don't defend yourself** or try to turn your partner's complaint around
Follow the rules for leveling and editing	**Don't get angry or withdraw** when you gripe
Listen and accept your partner's gripes	**Don't go "tit for tat"** or cross-complain when your partner raises a gripe. Be alert for speaker and listener filters

Table 13.2 Good and Bad Problem Definitions

Good problem definitions...	Bad problem definitions...
Are mutually agreed upon	State only one partner's view
Outline each partner's role in the problem	Are accusatory and blaming
Include a simple and specific description of the problem	Tend to be general and vague
Include a description of each partner's feelings	List each person's gripes about the problems
Include something positive	Focus only on the negative

Stage 3—Problem Solving

Gripe time turned general negative comments into specific concerns. Agenda building helped set priorities and one major issue was selected. If the couple ends up with more than one major issue, they should negotiate which issue will be discussed at that particular meeting, and the couple should schedule another meeting for the other issues.

In problem solving, the issue selected for discussion should be transformed into positive suggestions for change that are feasible and will remedy the problem. Problem solving for the couple involves the same specific steps as for the individual, but requires more negotiation, compromise, and give and take so that both partners feel that the solution works for them.

Exercise—Joint Problem Solving

Once the couple understands the basic structure and steps in the meeting and in the problem solving and contracting format, use the Family Meeting Worksheet in the workbook and choose a medium-level conflict issue to begin to role-play and shape the family meeting steps in the session. A sample Family Meeting Worksheet is shown in Figure 13.2. Have the couple complete the worksheet for homework. The couple should come up with an agreement that they think will work but should not implement it until it is discussed in next session.

Family Meeting Worksheet

Gripe Time—What do we have on our minds? <u>Finances, my daughter's upcoming visit</u>

Agenda Building—What is the one problem we should discuss today? <u>Finances</u>

Problem Solving:

1. Gather Information: <u>We both have bills and we keep our money separate, but it's not working.</u>

2. Problem Definition: <u>We don't have a livable budget that lets us save and pay our bills.</u>

3. Brainstorming for Solutions and Listing of Pros and Cons:

Solution	Pros (short and long term)	Cons (short and long term)
a. Open a joint checking account	Pools our money	Doesn't help us save
b. Have my partner pay all the bills and balance our checkbook	My partner is more responsible and will do a better job than I could	I may end up feeling like I have no control over our finances
c. Stop buying unnecessary items	Saves us money	Going shopping feels good
d. Start playing the lottery	Can win lots of money We can be set for life	Very unlikely to happen
e. Set aside a certain amount of money every month for savings	Saving money	May not have enough leftover for bills

4. Pick solution(s): <u>a, b, c, and e.</u>

5. Implement the solution for a period of time.

6. Reevaluate the solution—Did it work? <u>Look at our finances after 2 months to see if working.</u>

If not, do problem solving again

Figure 13.2
Example of Completed Family Meeting Worksheet

Identifying and Managing Warning Signs of Relapse (20 min)

Identifying Warning Signs

Introduce the concept of relapses and relapse prevention at this time.

Ask the couple to turn to the section on warning signs in Chapter 10 of the workbook and paraphrase the following:

The focus of our treatment has been on helping you achieve abstinence and then developing the skills you need to maintain abstinence in the long run. So far, you have been pretty successful with the treatment. (Adjust your introduction as necessary. If the client has had many slips, then refer to those. If the client has not had any slips, then introduce the possibility of future slips.)

However, we do know that many people who want to stay sober still have difficulties at times and may experience a slip or relapse. We have two more sessions after today, and we want to help you be prepared for situations you may face after treatment is over.

We will be focusing on relapses in two ways—first, by helping you identify warning signs of relapses, and developing some ways of trying to avoid the relapse, and second, by developing some strategies to think about and cope with slips in ways that should prevent full-blown relapses from occurring.

It may seem pessimistic to discuss drinking when you're not, but we like to think about relapse prevention the way we think about fire prevention—it is necessary to examine your home or office to try to eliminate fire hazards, but it's also necessary to have a fire extinguisher, fire drills, and the phone number of the fire department on hand!

Ask the couple for their reactions to this discussion.

Exercise—Identifying Warning Signs

After this introduction to relapse prevention, introduce the concept that there usually are "warning signs" that a relapse might be coming. These warning signs might be changes in the way the client is thinking or changes in behavior or habits.

Warning signs might be changes in the way either of you think and interact or changes in habits. You have learned many new behaviors. Through dedication, these behaviors can become everyday habits. Changes in these new habits may signal trouble. Look out for old habits, especially ones that led to trouble in the past. Look for changes in mood, people you associate with, places you go to, ways you handle problems, and routines. Be alert for changes in the way you think about alcohol, yourself, or things around you. All these things could signal the possibility of a slip.

Ask the client to think back to the last lapse or relapse that he experienced.

What kinds of thoughts, feelings, or behaviors occurred before the lapse that you now think were warning signs that a relapse might be coming?

Ask the couple to think about the period of time (several days) before the relapse, and identify any changes in the client's usual habits that they noticed, as well as his or her moods, people with whom the client was spending time, places that the client went, ways that the client handled problems or stressors, etc. Help the couple record the warning signs on the Identifying and Managing Relapse worksheet in the workbook.

Ask the couple to also think about any changes in the partner's behavior or mood during the same period of time before the client's latest relapse. Did the partner engage in counterproductive behaviors such as threatening or discussing past drinking? Did the partner act controlling in a drinking situation? Did the partner change any of his or her habits, moods, or people he or she was spending time with? Help the couple list the partner's warning signs on the worksheet as well.

Then, ask the couple to think about any ways that their interactions were different, in terms of arguments, the quality of their time together, or how they were handling problems. Again, help the couple list their shared warning signs on the worksheet.

After the couple has listed all warning signs, ask if there are any other experiences associated with past relapses that they think would be warning signs for future lapses or relapses.

Also point out that the couple has learned new ways of coping during therapy and that any changes away from the new behaviors might be warning signs. For homework, have each partner think about the new patterns he or she has established during therapy and what changes in these might be warning signs for relapse.

For example, the client might have initiated a regular exercise program after work at a time when he or she previously drank. Stopping the exercise program or beginning to skip workouts might be a subtle warning sign for impending relapse because the client would be beginning to fall back into old patterns.

Similarly, the couple might have begun to go out together regularly or have established a new pattern of talking over daily events while preparing dinner together. If they stopped these positive activities, that might be a warning sign. Refer to the notion of "seemingly irrelevant decisions" (see Session 9) and remind the couple that any changes in patterns that *seem* to have nothing to do with drinking may in fact set the client up to drink.

Managing Warning Signs for Relapse

Present the following rationale to the client:

> *We are going to continue to help you prepare to face situations that will occur after our treatment ends. Having a list of warning signs for relapses does not necessarily mean that you will be aware of them as warning signs when they actually occur—remember seemingly irrelevant decisions.* (Use the example of a client who stopped exercising, saying that he had hurt his back and couldn't do his usual workout, so he was going to wait until his back healed.)

Exercise—Managing Warnings Signs for Relapse

Go over the relapse warning signs that the client, partner, and couple identified on the completed Identifying and Managing Relapse Warning Signs worksheet. For one warning sign in each category, discuss a *plan* for what to do if that relapse warning sign should occur. Write down the plan in the space provided on the worksheet. For homework, ask the client, partner, and couple together to develop plans for the remaining warning signs listed.

Anticipating High-Risk Situations This Week (5 min)

Work with the client to identify at least one high-risk situation coming up in the next week (see sample dialogue in Session 1). Have the client write out ideas for handling the situation on the High-Risk Situations worksheet in the workbook. Remember to include the partner in this discussion.

Homework (5 min)

- Instruct the client to continue self-recording and record coping with high-risk situations on the back of the self-recording cards.

- Ask the client to complete one problem-solving exercise at home.

- Ask the couple to hold at least one family meeting, using the steps reviewed in the session and the homework.

- Instruct the partner to continue recording client's alcohol use and urges (intensity), and his or her own level of relationship satisfaction using the partner recording cards.

- Have the couple complete the Identifying and Managing Relapse Warning Signs worksheet.

- Have the couple read Chapter 10 of the workbook.

Chapter 14

Session 11: Relapse Prevention Part III / Acceptance Framework

(Corresponds to chapter 11 of the workbook)

Materials Needed

- Copy of couple's workbook
- Breathalyzer and 2 tubes
- Partner and client self-recording cards
- Alcohol Use and Urges and Relationship Satisfaction graphs in progress
- Plan for Handling Slips or Relapses worksheet
- Couple's Plan for Handling Slips or Relapses worksheet
- High-Risk Situations worksheet

Outline

- Determine blood alcohol level (BAL) of both the client and his or her partner
- Provide overview of session (5 min)
- Review self-recording and homework (5 min)
- Check in (5 min)
- Help the client develop a plan for handling slips and relapses (35 min)
- Discuss the importance of the partner's role in handling slips and relapses (10 min)

- Introduce to the couple how they might accept the things in one another that they don't necessarily like (20 min)
- Identify potential upcoming high-risk situations and plan for how to cope with them (5 min)
- Assign homework (5 min)

Blood Alcohol Level Determination

Reschedule if BAL of client or partner is greater than >.05. Check on compliance with homework and abstinence goal.

Overview of Session and Set Agenda (5 min)

Inform couple of topics that will be covered in the session. Ask the couple if there are any additional issues they would like to discuss today.

Review Self-Recording and Homework (5 min)

1. Review self-recording, update graphs, and give feedback and reinforcement.
2. Review application of other self-control procedures: Questions? Problems?
3. Review client's problem-solving homework.
4. Review client's warning signs homework.
5. Review partner's warning signs homework.
6. Review couple's warning signs homework.
7. Review Family Meeting Worksheet. Have couple plan another family meeting during the week to handle a more difficult problem or concern.

Check In (5 min)

Ask couple how their week was in general. Acknowledge both partners' concerns. Use information from this discussion for specific topics in the rest of the session.

Handling Slips and Relapses (35 min)

Offer the following rationale to the client:

Sometimes discussions of warning signs aren't enough—even using your best skills you may still have difficulties. It will be easier for you in the long run if you don't, but it is possible that you will eventually take a drink, despite your best efforts. If drinking occurs, it is important to realize that one drink does not have to inevitably lead to a full-blown relapse.

A person who slips can think of it in three ways:

1. *The slip is a mistake which should never be repeated. This is considered a lapse if the person does not continue drinking.*

2. *The slip is an opportunity to learn about something risky. The person should think of different ways to handle the situation in the future. This is considered a prolapse if the person does not continue drinking but learns a lesson for the future.*

3. *The slip is a disaster which shows that the person is hopeless. People who see the slip in this way think "I have blown it. I will never succeed. I will just give up."*

The third way of thinking is the worst choice. Slips are like falling off a bicycle. The fall may hurt, but you should get back on the bicycle and keep riding. You may feel rotten about the slip, but you should get back to remaining sober. The slip may even be an opportunity to learn about a difficult situation.

Review the information on the following page with the couple.

Looking for and thinking about warning signs help to prevent a slip. However, even people who work hard to remain abstinent may find themselves in an overwhelming situation. While you should work hard and expect to not take another drink, we believe you should be prepared for the possibility of a slip.

If you should take a drink, you have choices. As discussed previously, there are three different ways to think about the drink. You could think of it as a mistake (a slip), a mistake from which you learn something (a prolapse), or as a hopeless disaster (a relapse). The goal is never to have a relapse.

A drink does not have to become a relapse. If you ever have a drink, you should try to make it turn out to be a slip or prolapse. If you have a drink, remember the following:

1. **Don't panic.** One drink does not have to lead to an extended binge or a return to uncontrolled drinking.

2. **Stop, look, and listen.** Stop the ongoing flow of events and look and listen to what is happening. The lapse should be seen as a warning signal that the client or couple is in trouble. The lapse is like a flat tire—it is time to pull off the road to deal with the situation.

3. **Be aware of the abstinence violation effect.** Once you have a drink you may have thoughts such as "I blew it," or "All our efforts were a waste," or "As long as I've blown it, I might as well keep drinking," or "My willpower has failed, I have no control," or "I'm addicted, and once I drink my body will take over." These thoughts might be accompanied by feelings of anger or guilt. It is crucial to dispute these thoughts immediately.

4. **Renew your commitment.** After a lapse, it is easy to feel discouraged and to want to give up. Think back over the reasons why you decided to change your drinking in the first place; look at your decisional matrix and think about all the positive long-term benefits of abstinence and the long-term problems associated with continued drinking.

5. **Decide on a course of action.** At a minimum, this should include:

    - Getting out of the drinking situation.
    - Waiting at least two hours before having a second drink.
    - Engaging in some activity during those 2 hours that would help avoid continued drinking. The activity might be a pleasurable one, or reviewing materials from treatment, or talking over the lapse with someone who could be helpful, or calling your therapist.

6. **Review the situation leading up to the lapse.** Don't blame yourself for what happened. By focusing on your own failings, you will feel guiltier and blame yourself more. Ask yourself, what events led up to the slip? What were the main triggers? Were there any early warning signs? Did you try to deal with these constructively? If not, why not? Was your motivation weakened by fatigue, social pressure, or depression? Once you have analyzed the slip, think about what changes you need to make to avoid future slips.

7. **Ask for help.** Make it easier on yourself by asking someone to help you either by encouraging you, giving you advice, distracting you, or engaging in some alternative activity with you. If you had a flat tire and your spare tire also was flat, you'd have to get help—a slip is the same situation.

Exercise—Handling Slips and Relapses

Using the Plan for Handling Slips and Relapses worksheet in the workbook, discuss and have the client write down some plans for handling slips or relapses, should they occur. Use real-life examples of previously discussed high-risk situations, as well as possible anticipated, problematic situations that the client thinks might generate strong cravings and use of alcohol (i.e. accident or death in the family, loss of job, etc.).

A sample Plan for Handling Slips and Relapses worksheet is shown in Figure 14.1. This worksheet should be thought of as a "tool" the client can turn to and read in the event of a slip.

Plan for Handling Slips and Relapses

Immediate plans to prevent the slip from becoming a relapse:

Get out of the situation where I'm drinking. Pour what's left (if anything) down the drain or ask my partner to get rid of it.

Ask myself, "what was the trigger for my drinking in this particular situation?"

How I will get support to handle the relapse?

Tell my partner, talk to my sister

Call someone in AA or SMART Recovery

Call my therapist

The next day . . .

Review the information in my workbook.

Look at my negative consequences card.

Identify my triggers and deal with them.

Figure 14.1
Example of Completed Plan for Handling Slips and Relapses

Partner Role in Handling Slips and Relapses (10 min)

Begin this discussion with the following dialogue:

If drinking occurs, it is important that you know how to deal with it together. If you approach a slip the way you've learned to approach other problems, it will help you both get back on track more quickly. Open communication, use of X, Y, Z feedback, and good problem solving all can help.

Exercise—Handling Slips and Relapses Together

Using the Couple's Plan for Handling Slips or Relapses worksheet in the workbook, help the couple consider four issues:

1. What the client should do or say to the partner if he or she drinks, and how the partner could respond;

2. How the partner could initiate the conversation if he or she realizes that the client has had something to drink, and how the client could respond;

3. What steps they can take as a couple to respond to drinking; and

4. What, if any, limits the partner might place in terms of his or her response to drinking (for example, if the partner felt strongly that he or she would separate from the client if the client started drinking, the partner should make that clear).

Encourage the couple to discuss each of these possible scenarios, coming up with as specific a plan as possible for what to say or do. If there is time, the couple should role-play one discussion in the session.

Acceptance/Change Framework (20 min)

Therapist Note

■ *To gain an understanding of acceptance strategies in behavioral couple therapy, therapists should read:*

Dimidjian, S., Martell, C. R., & Christensen, A. (2002). Integrative behavioral couple therapy. In A. S. Gurman, & N. S. Jacobson (Eds.), *Clinical handbook of couple therapy* (3rd ed., pp. 251–280). New York, NY: Guilford Press. ∎

Previous sessions have focused on behaviors the couple wanted each other to change. It also may be possible for the partners to think about something they don't like about their partner in a new way. An alternative perspective to wanting the behavior to change is to view it as understandable, as something different to be appreciated, or at least as something to be accepted and tolerated. Increasing one partner's tolerance for the other person's behavior will reduce the distress caused by that behavior. The key to building tolerance is to give up the struggle to change the other partner and to experience the behavior in a context in which acceptance is promoted. Examples of behaviors that partners may be able to learn to tolerate are the amount of distance/closeness desired, different preferences in terms of activities to do together, and different levels of sexual desire.

> *We have discussed various behaviors you have each wanted the other to change. Each of you does things that the other doesn't like, and each of you wishes the other would do some things that the other does not do. (Give specific examples that have been addressed or discussed during the therapy.)*

> *We have been working in the last few sessions on ways to tell each other what upsets you and requesting change. Today, we are going to discuss a different approach. We are going to explore whether there are some that you could learn to accept. We know that people are package deals—they have wonderful qualities that you love, and some not so wonderful qualities. No one is perfect! If you can build up your ability to accept a previously upsetting behavior, you will find that it will be less painful for you. The key to building tolerance is to give up the struggle to change your partner. We are going to work on situations in which you may be able to **accept** behavior which previously upset you.*

Exercise—Building Acceptance

Ask each partner to identify a behavior he or she has viewed negatively but that the partner simply has never changed. Ask him or her if he or she can identify positive aspects to the behavior. It may be possible to frame that negative behavior as part of a characteristic that originally attracted or now attracts the partner. You can also note that individual differences create balance in the relationship so it can function more smoothly.

For homework, ask the couple to do the same exercise with another of their partner's behaviors that they have traditionally viewed in a negative manner.

Anticipating High-Risk Situations This Week (5 min)

Work with the client to identify at least one high-risk situation coming up in the next week (see sample dialogue in Session 1). Have the client write out ideas for handling the situation on the High-Risk Situations worksheet in the workbook. Remember to include the partner in this discussion.

Homework (5 min)

- Instruct the client to continue self-recording and record coping with high-risk situations on the back of the client self-recording cards.

- Have the client draft plans for slips or relapses by situation.

- Have the couple complete the Couple's Plan for Handling Slips or Relapses worksheet, and role-play one scenario at home.

- Ask the client to think about one characteristic of his or her partner that he or she will focus on learning to accept.

✏ Instruct the partner to continue recording the client's alcohol use and urges (intensity), and his or her own level of relationship satisfaction using the partner recording cards.

✏ Ask the partner to think about one characteristic of his or her partner that he or she will focus on learning to accept.

✏ Have the couple read Chapter 11 of the workbook.

Chapter 15 Session 12: Review / Relapse Prevention Part IV

(Corresponds to chapter 12 of the workbook)

Materials Needed

- Copy of couple's workbook
- Breathalyzer and 2 tubes
- Alcohol Use and Urges and Relationship Satisfaction graphs in progress
- Relapse Contract

Session Outline

- Determine blood alcohol level (BAL) of both the client and his or her partner
- Provide overview of session (5 min)
- Review self-recording and homework (5 min)
- Check in (5 min)
- Review techniques and plan for maintaining treatment gains (40 min)
- Develop a relapse prevention contract (25 min)

Blood Alcohol Level Determination

Reschedule if BAL of client or partner is greater than >.05. Check on compliance with homework and abstinence goal.

Overview of Session and Set Agenda (5 min)

Inform couple of topics that will be covered in the session. Ask the couples if there are any additional issues they would like to discuss today.

Review Self-Recording and Homework (5 min)

After setting today's agenda, review the couple's completed self-recording cards, update progress graphs, and provide feedback and reinforcement to client. Spend a few minutes reviewing and discussing the trajectory of the graphs. Give positive feedback to the client for reducing the frequency and intensity of cravings, as well as drinking. Show the client how the graph reflects how much different his drinking habits are now versus what they were at the beginning of treatment. Remind the client of how difficult it was in the first few weeks of treatment when cravings were frequent and strong. The client can look to this graph for encouragement in the future, if and when cravings occur.

Review graph of relationship satisfaction. If satisfaction has increased, or was high and remained high, comment on the positive relationship that the couples has. If satisfaction remains fairly low, comment on the work that still needs to be done, emphasizing that the treatment has provided them with a number of skills to use in the coming months.

Review other homework:

1. Couple's Plan for Handling Slips or Relapses worksheet and role-play at home.

2. Client and partner homework to identify a characteristic of the other to focus on learning to accept.

Check In (5 min)

Ask couple how their week was in general. Acknowledge both partners' concerns. Use information from this for specific topics in the rest of the session.

Final Review and Maintenance Planning (40 min)

The goal of this session is to give the couple a positive set or expectancy that the client now has the skills to remain abstinent, the partner has better ways to cope with issues related to drinking, and the couple has begun to learn how to have a happier relationship. In addition, the goal is to let the couple know that they have learned a set of skills that can be applied in the day-to-day environment to deal with high-risk situations and that relapse-prevention techniques will help the client maintain gains made during treatment. The learning of these skills has placed control back into the client's hands.

Client Skills

Review the following self-control skills the client has learned:

1. Self-recording
2. Functional analysis (behavior chains)
3. Self-management planning
4. Cognitive self-control procedures
5. Positive alternatives to drinking
6. Relapse-prevention strategies

Have the client identify the skills that he or she thinks have been most important to the changes made during therapy. Explore the strategies and techniques that the client will continue to try to implement in order to maintain progress, now that treatment is ending. If the client wants to continue therapy or feels the need to come back in the future, discuss his or her options.

Inform the client that he or she will most probably continue to experience urges to drink periodically. Daily self-recording should be continued. Remind the client that relapses most often occur in the type of situations he or she is now prepared to handle.

Partner Skills

Review the following skills the partner has learned to cope with drinking:

1. Support
2. Ways to decrease triggers for the client's drinking
3. Ways to protect the client less from negative consequences of drinking
4. How to support the client when he or she has urges to drink or when he or she is in an awkward situation with alcohol present

Have the partner identify the skills he or she thinks have been most important. Explore how the partner can continue these positive changes.

Couple Skills

Review the following skills the couple has learned to build a better relationship:

1. Focusing on positive actions ("Notice Something Nice")
2. Sharing activities together and focusing on making the experience positive for each other
3. Learning more about good communication
4. Learning how to solve problems together
5. Learning to accept each other more

Have the couple identify the most important changes they have made. Discuss how they can continue these positive changes.

Relapse Contract (25 min)

Using the template provided, work with the couple to create a relapse contract. Include ways to address the possible relapse warning signs and ways of handling those that they each have identified. Review in detail the emergency plan for relapse, including actions to be taken. Have both partners sign the contract.

Sample Relapse Contract

1. If I drink alcohol at all, in any amount, I will sit down the following day and review what to do in the event of a relapse. I will use my trigger sheets to figure out what happened. I will tell my partner and ask for his or her support.

2. If I drink again within a month, I will call my therapist with the goal of getting a referral to get back into treatment.

3. If I drink even once in a binge (out of control) fashion, I will call, with the goal of getting back into treatment.

4. My goal is to remain abstinent for at least _____.
   At that time I will re-evaluate this contract and write a new one.

_____   _____
Client Signature   Date

1. If _____ drinks, I will ask how I can help him or her. I will not yell.

2. If he or she keeps drinking, I will suggest that we call to get more treatment.

3. If he or she refuses help and keeps drinking, I will call for help for myself.

_____   _____
Partner Signature   Date

_____   _____
Therapist Signature   Date

Wrap-Up

Congratulate the couple on the work they have done, encourage them to maintain changes, and tell them to give you a call if they have questions or concerns in the future.

Drinking Patterns Questionnaire

We have found that each person has a unique or different pattern of drinking alcohol. People drink more at certain times of the day, in particular moods, with certain people, in specific places, and so forth. It is very common for people to drink more under various stresses, before or after difficult interactions, and when they are experiencing particular feelings. It may sometimes seem that there are no circumstances that relate to your drinking, that is, "I just drink." However, after some thought, every person can identify at least some important factors.

This questionnaire will help you to think about different aspects of your life and how each might relate to your drinking. You will find instructions at the beginning of each section. Please give each item careful consideration. You will benefit most from this questionnaire if you are honest and open with your responses.

For each item, mark with an "X" whether or not you drank in this situation in the *PAST 6 MONTHS*.

Use the following options to answer each of the questions:

- Mark "X" under **Did not drink** if you did not drink in this situation in the past 6 months.

- Mark "X" under **Sometimes drank** if you did drink in this situation in the past 6 months.

- Mark "X" under **Major drinking**, if you drank often in this situation in the past 6 months.

Section 1: Environmental Factors Related to Drinking

Various locations, times, people, activities, and events are associated with every person's drinking. The items in this section will help you to think about these factors. Read each item carefully as some are divided into more than one part.

Location

Put an "X" in one box next to each of the following items to indicate the frequency with which you drank in each of the following locations during the *PAST 6 MONTHS*. If the location does not apply to you, answer "Did not drink in this location."

	Drinking locations	Did not drink in this location	Sometimes drank in this location	Major drinking location
1.	Home			
2.	Bar			
3.	Club			
4.	Private club			
5.	Automobile			
6.	Outdoors			
7.	Church or temple			
8.	Work			
9.	Restaurant			
10.	Other's home			

After you have answered each of the above questions, go back and put a circle around the number of the location where you drank *most* often during the *past 6 months*.

Time

Put an "X" in one box next to each of the following items to indicate the frequency with which you drank at each of the following times during the *PAST 6 MONTHS*. If the time does not apply to you, answer "Did not drink at this time."

	Drinking times	Did not drink at this time	Sometimes drank at this time	Major drinking time
11.	During the morning			
12.	Lunchtime			
13.	Afternoon			
14.	After work (if employed)			
15.	During supper			
16.	During the evening			
17.	At bedtime			
18.	During the night			

After you have answered each of the above questions, go back and put a circle around the number of the time during which you drank *most* often during the *past 6 months*.

Companions

Put an "X" in one box next to each of the following items to indicate the frequency with which you drank with each of the following people during the *PAST 6 MONTHS*. If a particular person does not apply to you, answer "Did not drink with this person."

	Drinking companions	**Did not drink with this person**	**Sometimes drank with this person**	**Major drinking companion**
19.	Spouse/Partner			
20.	Relative			
21.	Child			
22.	Male friend(s)			
23.	Female friend(s)			
24.	Male and female friend(s)			
25.	Alone			
26.	Strangers			
27.	Business acquaintances			

After you have answered each of the above questions, go back and put a circle around the number of the person with whom you drank *most* often during the *past 6 months*.

Activities

Put an "X" in one box next to each of the following items to indicate the frequency with which you drank during each of the following activities during the *PAST 6 MONTHS*. If a particular activity does not apply to you, answer "Did not drink during this activity."

	Drinking activities	Did not drink during this activity	Sometimes drank during this activity	Major drinking activity
28.	Cooking			
29.	Chores			
30.	Shopping			
31.	Smoking			
32.	Watching television			
33.	Eating			
34.	Reading			
35.	Resting			
36.	Doing crafts or hobby			
37.	Talking			
38.	Playing pool			
39.	Playing games (cards, pinball, etc.)			
40.	Gambling (horses, dogs)			
41.	Entertaining			
42.	Listening to entertainment			

continued

continued

	Drinking activities	Did not drink during this activity	Sometimes drank during this activity	Major drinking activity
43.	Attending a meeting			
44.	Partying			
45.	Driving			
46.	Playing sports			
47.	Attending sporting event			
48.	Sunbathing			
49.	Cooking out			
50.	Walking or hiking			
51.	Recreational activities (fishing, swimming, etc.)			
52.	In sexual activities			
53.	Fighting (arguing)			

After you have answered each of the above questions, go back and put a circle around the number of the activity during which you drank *most* often during the *past 6 months*.

Urges

Put an "X" in one box next to each of the following items that best describes your drinking or urges to drink during the *PAST 6 MONTHS*. If a particular situation does not apply to you, answer "Did not drink in this situation."

	Drinking urges	Did not drink in this situation	Sometimes drank in this situation	Major drinking situation
54.	I sometimes drink when I see or hear an advertisement for alcohol (TV commercial, magazine ad, billboard, etc.)			
55.	I sometimes drink when passing a particular bar or restaurant			
56.	I sometimes drink when I see someone else drinking			
57.	I sometimes drink when I hear people talking about drinking			
58.	I seem to drink more on particular days of the week			
59.	I seem to drink more during certain times of the month			
60.	I seem to drink more at certain times of the year (holidays, vacations, etc.)			

continued

continued

	Drinking urges	Did not drink in this situation	Sometimes drank in this situation	Major drinking situation
61.	I sometimes like to have a drink with certain foods, snacks, or meals			
62.	When I drink at home, I usually drink only in certain parts of the house			
63.	I sometimes drink more frequently in certain types of weather (hot day, cold day, etc.)			

After you have answered each of the above questions, go back and put a circle around the number of the situation during which you drank *most* often during the *past 6 months*.

Section 2: Work Related

Put an "X" in one box next to each of the following items to indicate *YES* or *NO*, whether each of the following three items applied to you in the *PAST 6 MONTHS*.

		YES	NO
A	I have been employed at some time in the PAST 6 MONTHS		
B	I have done volunteer work in the PAST 6 MONTHS		
C	I have looked for work in the PAST 6 MONTHS		

If you did *not* answer "Yes" to A, B, or C above, skip the entire "Work" section (questions 64–76).

If you *did* answer "Yes" to either item A, B, or C, please complete the entire "Work" section.

It is not unusual at times for people to drink because of work-related events or difficulties. This can happen in both paying jobs and volunteer work. The stress of looking for a job may also relate to drinking. Put an "X" in the box next to each of the following items that best describes your drinking in the *PAST 6 MONTHS*.

		Did not drink in this situation	**Sometimes drank in this situation**	**Major drinking situation**
64.	I sometimes drink before I go to work			
65.	I sometimes drink on the job			

continued

continued

		Did not drink in this situation	**Sometimes drank in this situation**	**Major drinking situation**
66.	I sometimes drink during work breaks			
67.	I sometimes go drinking with friends straight from work before stopping home			
68.	I sometimes drink after work to help relieve some of the pressure from the job			
69.	I sometimes drink with business associates at meetings, conventions, cocktail parties, etc.			
70.	I sometimes drink when I have problems with my co-workers or boss			
71.	I sometimes drink when I get nervous at work			
72.	I sometimes drink when I feel that I'm not getting anywhere in my job or career			
73.	I sometimes drink when I am happy with the way work is going			
74.	I sometimes drink more on payday after cashing my check			

continued

		Did not drink in this situation	**Sometimes drank in this situation**	**Major drinking situation**
75.	I sometimes drink after a job interview			
76.	I sometimes drink when I feel that finding a new job is hopeless			

After you have answered each of the above questions, go back and put a circle around the number of the situation during which you drank *most* often during the *past 6 months*.

Section 3: Financial

Often, people drink as a response to financial difficulties. For each of the following items put an "X" in the box that best describes your drinking in the *PAST 6 MONTHS*. If a particular situation does not apply to you, put an "X" under "Did not drink in this situation."

		Did not drink in this situation	**Sometimes drank in this situation**	**Major drinking situation**
77.	I sometimes drink when I attempt to pay my bills and I get frustrated			
78.	I sometimes drink when I worry about my finances			
79.	I sometimes drink when I feel bad or guilty about not being a good provider			
80.	I sometimes drink when I can't buy something that a family member requests			
81.	I sometimes drink when I can't afford something that I want very much			
82.	I sometimes drink when a family member makes a purchase that I know we can't afford			
83.	I sometimes drink after I spend too much money			

continued

		Did not drink in this situation	**Sometimes drank in this situation**	**Major drinking situation**
84.	I sometimes drink when I think that my spouse doesn't make enough money			
85.	I sometimes feel like drinking because of arguments over how to spend money			
86.	I sometimes drink when I get angry over who controls the money			
87.	I sometimes am more tempted to drink when my finances are going well and/or I have caught up with all of my bills			
88.	I am sometimes more tempted to drink when I have a lot of money in my pocket			

After you have answered each of the above questions, go back and put a circle around the number of the situation during which you drank *most* often during the *past 6 months*.

Section 4: Physiological

Put an "X" in one box next to each of the following items that best describes your drinking behavior during the *PAST 6 MONTHS*. If a particular situation does not apply to you, put an "X" in the box that indicates "Did not drink in this situation."

		Did not drink in this situation	Sometimes drank in this situation	Major drinking situation
89.	I sometimes feel shaky and drink to stop it			
90.	I sometimes drink when I feel tired or fatigued			
91.	I sometimes drink when I get restless			
92.	I sometimes drink when I'm experiencing physical pain (back pain, headache, etc.)			
93.	I sometimes take a drink if I have trouble falling asleep			
94.	I sometimes wake up during the night and take a drink to get back to sleep			
95.	I sometimes drink alcohol when I am thirsty			
96.	I sometimes drink before my menstrual period			

After you have answered each of the above questions, go back and put a circle around the number of the situation during which you drank *most* often during the *past 6 months*.

Section 5: Interpersonal

People drink in social situations, that is, with other people, for many reasons. Put an "X" in one box next to each of the following items that best describes your drinking in the *PAST 6 MONTHS*. If a particular situation does not apply to you, put an "X" under "Did not drink in this situation."

		Did not drink in this situation	Sometimes drank in this situation	Major drinking situation
97.	It is sometimes difficult for me not to drink when people around me are drinking			
98.	I sometimes find it hard to resist if someone buys me a drink or offers to do so			
99.	I sometimes drink to be part of the group			
100.	I sometimes drink as a way to meet people or be with others			
101.	I sometimes drink to feel more comfortable with others			
102.	I sometimes think that I don't relate well to others and drinking helps me do so			
103.	I sometimes feel that I'm not as good as other people and drinking helps me feel better			

continued

continued

		Did not drink in this situation	**Sometimes drank in this situation**	**Major drinking situation**
104.	I sometimes find that I drink after I become angry at someone			
105.	I sometimes drink after feeling hurt by someone			
106.	I sometimes drink when I want to hurt or get back at someone			
107.	I sometimes drink when I am angry at myself for not speaking my mind to someone			
108.	I sometimes drink to help me express my feelings towards someone (anger, love, etc.)			
109.	I sometimes drink when I feel lonely			
110.	I sometimes drink because I think it's the only way to have fun			
111.	I sometimes drink when I'm bored and have nothing to do			
112.	I sometimes drink when I think that nobody cares about me			

continued

		Did not drink in this situation	**Sometimes drank in this situation**	**Major drinking situation**
113.	I sometimes drink when I want someone to pay attention to me			
114.	I sometimes drink when I feel that people have put too much responsibility on me			
115.	I sometimes drink when I think about past relationships			

After you have answered each of the above questions, go back and put a circle around the number of the situation during which you drank *most* often during the *past 6 months*.

Section 6: Marital/Relationship

Put an "X" in the YES or NO box to indicate whether you have been married or involved in a romantic relationship in the *PAST 6 MONTHS*:

	YES	NO
I have been married or involved in a romantic relationship in the past 6 months		

If you answered "NO" to this question, skip the entire "Marital/Relationship" section (questions 116–142).

If you answered "Yes" to this question, please complete the entire "Marital/Relationship" section.

Although sometimes hard to discuss, it is quite common for relationship issues to be related to drinking. Put an "X" in the box after each of the following items that best describes your drinking in the *PAST 6 MONTHS*. If a particular situation does not apply to you, put an "X" under "Did not drink in this situation."

		Did not drink in this situation	Sometimes drank in this situation	Major drinking situation
116.	I sometimes drink when I anticipate an argument with my partner			
117.	I sometimes drink after having an argument with my partner			
118.	I sometimes drink after my partner nags me about something			

continued

		Did not drink in this situation	Sometimes drank in this situation	Major drinking situation
119.	I sometimes drink after my partner criticizes me			
120.	I sometimes drink when my partner is drinking or offers me a drink			
121.	I sometimes drink to help me express my feelings toward my partner			
122.	I sometimes drink when my partner and I are celebrating something			
123.	I sometimes drink after my partner and I disagree about sexual relations			
124.	I sometimes drink or get an urge to drink when I want to avoid sexual relations with my partner			
125.	I sometimes drink when I'm concerned about my sexual adequacy			
126.	I sometimes drink when I want to enjoy sexual relations more			
127.	I sometimes drink after physical violence occurs in the family or when I have concerns about it			

continued

continued

		Did not drink in this situation	Sometimes drank in this situation	Major drinking situation
128.	I sometimes drink when I think my partner or family doesn't care about me			
129.	I sometimes drink when I feel that my partner doesn't understand my needs or desires			
130.	I sometimes drink when my partner doesn't spend enough time with me			
131.	I sometimes drink when I feel "trapped" in my relationship			
132.	I sometimes drink when I'm frustrated that my partner and I can't resolve a conflict			
133.	I sometimes drink after my partner embarrasses me in public			
134.	I sometimes drink at times when I am jealous			
135.	I sometimes drink when my partner and I have conflict on how to deal with our child(ren)			
136.	I sometimes drink when I am not happy with my role in the family			
137.	I sometimes drink when it seems that my partner is not treating my like an adult			

continued

		Did not drink in this situation	**Sometimes drank in this situation**	**Major drinking situation**
138.	I sometimes drink when I think my partner is too involved with my affairs			
139.	I sometimes drink when I feel that my partner doesn't meet his or her responsibilities			
140.	I sometimes drink when I feel that I don't meet my responsibilities			
141.	I sometimes drink to "get back" at my partner			
142.	I sometimes drink more when my partner tries to stop my drinking			

After you have answered each of the above questions, go back and put a circle around the number of the situation during which you drank *most* often during the *past 6 months*.

Section 7: Parents

Put an "X" in the YES or NO box to indicate whether at least one of your parents and/or in-laws are still living:

		YES	NO
A	My parents are still living		
B	My in-laws are still living		

If you answered "No" to both A and B, skip the entire "Parents" section (questions 143–154).

If you answered "Yes" to either A or B, please complete the entire "Parents" section.

Put an "X" in one box that best describes your drinking in the *PAST 6 MONTHS*. If a particular situation does not apply to you, put an "X" under "Did not drink in this situation."

		Did not drink in this situation	Sometimes drank in this situation	Major drinking situation
143.	I sometimes drink with my parents or in-laws			
144.	I sometimes drink after spending time with my parents or in-laws			
145.	I sometimes drink to help me express my feelings towards my parents or in-laws			
146.	I sometimes drink when I'm upset with my parents or in-laws			

continued

		Did not drink in this situation	Sometimes drank in this situation	Major drinking situation
147.	I sometimes drink when I feel that my parents or in-laws don't respect me as an adult			
148.	I sometimes drink when I feel guilty about something related to my parents or in-laws			
149.	I sometimes drink when I hurt or embarrass my parents or in-laws			
150.	I sometimes drink when I feel that my parents or in-laws are too demanding or interfering			
151.	I sometimes drink after my parents or in-laws and I disagree about something			
152.	I sometimes drink when I think about things that my parents did to me when I was younger			
153.	I sometimes drink when I see that my parents or in-laws are getting older			
154.	I sometimes drink when I think about the death of one or both of my parents or in-laws			

After you have answered each of the above questions, go back and put a circle around the number of the situation during which you drank *most* often during the *past 6 months*.

Section 8: Children

If you have children, interactions with your children can lead you to certain feelings or moods related to your drinking. Put an "X" under the *YES* or *NO* box to indicate whether you have any children.

YES	NO

If you do *not* have any children, skip the remainder of this section (questions 155–171).

Please complete this section even if children from your present or previous marriage are not currently living with you. Put an "X" after each of the following items for the *PAST 6 MONTHS*. If a particular situation does not apply to you, put an "X" under "Did not drink in this situation."

		Did not drink in this situation	Sometimes drank in this situation	Major drinking situation
155.	I sometimes drink after interacting with my children			
156.	I sometimes drink when my spouse and I have a disagreement about our children			
157.	I sometimes drink to help me express my feelings toward my children			

continued

		Did not drink in this situation	Sometimes drank in this situation	Major drinking situation
158.	I sometimes drink when I'm annoyed with my children			
159.	I sometimes drink when I feel that my children don't respect me			
160.	I sometimes drink when I feel that my children are ashamed of me			
161.	I sometimes drink after my children get in trouble at school or with legal authorities			
162.	I sometimes drink after my children do not follow my orders or wishes			
163.	I sometimes drink when I feel that my children are too much responsibility			
164.	I sometimes drink when I feel that I cannot control my children			
165.	I sometimes drink when I feel guilty about something related to my children			
166.	I sometimes drink when I can't give my children something they want			

continued

continued

		Did not drink in this situation	Sometimes drank in this situation	Major drinking situation
167.	I sometimes drink after punishing my children too harshly or losing my temper			
168.	I sometimes drink after my children manipulate my spouse/partner into doing something with which I'm not pleased			
169.	I sometimes drink when I want to see my children but I can't do so			
170.	I sometimes drink when my children talk back to me			
171.	I sometimes drink when I feel that my children don't need me any longer			

After you have answered each of the above questions, go back and put a circle around the number of the situation during which you drank *most* often during the *past 6 months*.

Section 9: Emotional

People often drink when they are experiencing some type of emotion, either negative or positive. Put an "X" next to each emotion on the following list to describe the emotions you have or haven't experienced before drinking in the *PAST 6 MONTHS*. If a particular emotion does not apply to you, put an "X" under "Did not drink with this emotion."

		Did not drink with this emotion	Sometimes drank in this situation	Major drinking-related emotion
172.	Angry			
173.	Sad			
174.	Depressed			
175.	Hurt			
176.	Spiteful			
177.	Lonely			
178.	Hopeless			
179.	Frustrated			
180.	Guilty			
181.	Fearful			
182.	Nervous			

continued

continued

		Did not drink with this emotion	**Sometimes drank in this situation**	**Major drinking-related emotion**
183	Restless			
184	Insecure			
185	Fatigued			
186	Happy			
187	Relaxed			
188	Self-confident			
189.	Loving			

After you have answered each of the above questions, go back and put a circle around the number of the feeling with which you drank *most* often during the *past 6 months*.

Review

You have now finished the sections of the questionnaire dealing with events, people, and feelings that come before your drinking or urges to drink. We would like you to look back over the questionnaire and think about the relative importance of each of these sections as it applies to your drinking, that is, how important each section is compared to the other sections.

The different sections of the questionnaire that you have just completed are listed below. Think about the section that is most important, out of all nine sections, in relation to your drinking or urges to drink. Put an "X" under "1" next to that section. Then think about the section that is second most important to your drinking, and put an "X" under "2" next to that section. Then think about the section that is third most important to your drinking, and put an "X" under "3" next to that section. Continue to do that until you have ranked each of the nine sections listed below. Each number should be used only once. The sections marked "8" and "9" should be least important related to your drinking, compared to the other sections.

Most Important- -Least Important

		1	2	3	4	5	6	7	8	9
Section 1	Environmental (p. 234)									
Section 2	Work (p. 241)									
Section 3	Financial (p. 244)									
Section 4	Physiological (p. 246)									
Section 5	Interpersonal (p. 247)									
Section 6	Marital/ Relationship (p. 250)									
Section 7	Parents (p. 254)									
Section 8	Children (p. 256)									
Section 9	Emotional (p. 259)									

References

Allen, J. P., & Litten, R. Z. (2001). The role of laboratory tests in alcoholism treatment. *Journal of Substance Abuse Treatment, 20*, 81–85.

American Psychiatric Association. (2004). *Diagnostic and statistical manual of mental disorders: DSM-IV-TR* (4th ed., text revision). Washington, DC: Author.

Anton, R. F., O'Malley, S. S., Ciraulo, D. A., Cisler, R. A., Couper, D., Donovan, D. M., et al. COMBINE Study Research Group. (2006). Combined pharmacotherapies and behavioral interventions for alcohol dependence: The COMBINE study: A randomized controlled trial. *The Journal of the American Medical Association, 295*(17), 2003–2017.

Armor, D. J., Polich, J. M., & Stambul, H. B. (1978). *Alcoholism and treatment.* New York, NY: John Wiley & Sons.

Barber, W. S., & O'Brien, C. P. (1999). Pharmacotherapies. In B. S. McCrady, & E. E. Epstein (Eds.), *Addictions: A comprehensive guidebook* (pp. 347–369). New York, NY: Oxford University Press.

Bates, M. E., Bowden, S. C., & Barry, D. (2002). Neurocognitive impairment associated with alcohol use disorders: Implications for treatment. *Experimental and Clinical Psychopharmacology, 10*, 193–212.

Beck, A. T., Epstein, N., Brown, G., & Steer, R. A. (1988). An inventory for measuring clinical anxiety: Psychometric properties. *Journal of Consulting and Clinical Psychology, 56*(6), 893–889.

Beck, A. T., Steer, R. A., & Garbin, M. G. (1988). Psychometric properties of the Beck Depression Inventory: Twenty-five years of evaluation. *Clinical Psychology Review, 8*(1), 77–100.

Busby, D. M., Christensen, C., Crane, D. R., & Larson, J. H. (1995). A revision of the Dyadic Adjustment Scale for use with distressed and nondistressed couples: Construct hierarchy and multidimensional scales. *Journal of Marital and Family Therapy, 21*, 289–308.

Carroll, K. (1999). Behavioral and cognitive behavioral treatments. In B. S. McCrady, & E. E. Epstein (Eds.), *Addictions: A comprehensive guidebook* (pp. 250–267). New York, NY: Oxford University Press.

Copello, A. G., Templeton, L. B., & Velleman, R. B. (2006). Family interventions for drug and alcohol misuse: Is there a best practice? *Current Opinion in Psychiatry, 19*(3), 271–276.

Drapkin, M. L., McCrady, B. S., Swingle, J. M., & Epstein, E. E. (2005). Exploring bidirectional couple violence in a clinical sample of female alcoholics. *Journal of Studies on Alcohol, 66,* 213–219.

Epstein, E. E., McCrady, B. S., Drapkin, M., & Cook, S. M. (2005, June). *Prognostic value of baseline psychopathology comorbid with alcohol dependence among women in outpatient treatment.* Presented at the Annual Meeting of the Research Society on Alcoholism, Santa Barbara, CA.

Epstein, E. E., & McCrady, B. S. (2002). Marital therapy in the treatment of alcohol problems. In: A. S. Gurman, & N. A. Jacobson (Eds.), *Clinical handbook of marital therapy* (3rd ed.)(pp. 597–628). New York, NY: Guilford Press.

Fals-Stewart, W., O'Farrell, T. J., Birchler, G., Cordova, J., & Kelley, M. L. (2005). Behavioral couples therapy for alcoholism and drug abuse: Where we've been, where we are, and where we're going. *Journal of Cognitive Psychotherapy, 19,* 229–246.

Finney, J. W., Moos, R. H., & Timko, C. (1999). The course of treated and untreated substance use disorders: Remission and resolution, relapse and mortality. In B. S. McCrady, & E. E. Epstein (Eds.), *Addictions: A comprehensive guidebook* (pp. 30–49). New York, NY: Oxford University Press.

First, M. B., Gibbon, M., Spitzer, R. L, & Williams, J. B. W. (1997). *The Structured Clinical Interview for DSM-IV: Axis II personality disorders (SCID-II)* Arlington, VA. American Psychiatric Press.

First, M. B., Spitzer, R. L., Gibbon, M., & Williams, J. B. W. (2002). *Structured clinical interview for the DSM-IV-TR: Axis I disorders, research version, patient edition (SCID-I/P).* New York, NY: Biometrics Research, New York State Psychiatric Institute.

Folstein, M. F., Folstein, S. E., & McHugh, P. R. (1975). Mini-mental state: A practical method for grading the cognitive state of patients for the clinician. *Journal of Psychiatric Research, 12,* 189–198.

Gottman, J. M., Notarius, C., Gonso, J., & Markman, H. (1976). *A couples guide to communication.* Champaign, IL: Research Press.

Grant, B. F., Dawson, D. A., Stinson, F. S., Chou, S. P., Dufour, M. C., & Pickering, R. P. (2004). The 12-month prevalence and trends in DSM-IV alcohol abuse and dependence: United States, 1991–1992 and 2001–2002. *Drug and Alcohol Dependence, 74*, 223–234.

Green, K. E., Pugh, L. A., McCrady, B. S., & Epstein, E. E. (2008). Unique aspects of female-primary alcoholic relationships. *Addictive Disorders and Their Treatment, 7, 169–176*.

Hall, S. M., Havassy, B. E., & Wasserman, D. A. (1991). Effects of commitment to abstinence, positive moods, stress, and coping on relapse to cocaine use. *Journal of Consulting & Clinical Psychology, 59*, 526–532.

Harwood, H. (2000). *Updating estimates of the economic costs of alcohol abuse in the United States: Estimates, update methods, and data*. Report prepared by The Lewin Group for the National Institute on Alcohol Abuse and Alcoholism.

Hedberg, A. G., & Campbell, L. (1974). A comparison of four behavioral treatments of alcoholism. *Journal of Behavior Therapy and Experimental Psychiatry, 5*, 251–256.

Hester, R. K. (2003). Behavioral self-control training. In R. K. Hester, & W. R. Miller (Eds.), *Handbook of alcoholism treatment approaches. Effective alternatives* (3rd ed., pp. 152–164). Boston, MA: Allyn & Bacon.

Kadden, R., Carroll, K., Donovan, D., Cooney, N., Monti, P., Abrams, D., et al. (1995). *Cognitive-behavioral coping skills therapy manual*. NIH Pub. No. 94-3724. Rockville, MD: National Institute on Alcohol Abuse and Alcoholism.

Kadden, R. M., & Skerker, P. M. (1999). Treatment decision making and goal setting. In B. S. McCrady, & E. E. Epstein (Eds.), *Addictions: A comprehensive guidebook* (pp. 216–231). New York, NY: Oxford University Press.

Kelley, M. L., & Fals-Stewart, W. (2002). Couples-versus individual-based therapy for alcohol and drug abuse: Effects on children's psychosocial functioning. *Journal of Consulting and Clinical Psychology, 70*, 417–427.

Longabaugh, R., Wirtz, P. W., Zweben, A., & Stout, R. L. (1998). Network support for drinking, Alcoholics Anonymous and long-term matching effects. *Addiction, 93*, 1313–1333.

Margolin, G., Talovic, S., & Weinstein, C. D. (1983). Areas of Change Questionnaire: A practical approach to marital assessment. *Journal of Consulting and Clinical Psychology, 51*, 921–931.

Marlatt, G. A., & Gordon, J. (1985). *Relapse prevention: Maintenance strategies in the treatment of addictive behaviors.* New York, NY: Guilford Press.

McCrady, B. S. (2007). Alcohol use disorders. In D. H. Barlow (Ed.), *Clinical handbook of psychological disorders* (4th ed., pp. 492–546). New York, NY: Guilford Publications.

McCrady, B. S., Epstein, E. E., & Cook. S. (2003, June). *Predicting change in women's drinking: Outcomes 12 months after treatment.* Presented at the Annual Meeting of the Research Society on Alcoholism, Ft. Lauderdale, FL.

McCrady, B. S., Epstein, E. E., & Cook, S. (2006, June). *What do women want? Characteristics of women choosing individual or couple therapy for alcohol problems.* Poster Presented at the Annual Meeting of the Research Society on Alcoholism, Baltimore, MD.

McCrady, B. S., Epstein, E. E., Cook, S., Jensen, N. K., & Hildebrandt, T. (under review). A randomized trial of individual and couple behavioral alcohol treatment for women.

McCrady, B. S., Epstein, E. E., & Kahler, C. W. (2004). AA and relapse prevention as maintenance strategies after conjoint behavioral alcohol treatment for men: 18 month outcomes. *Journal of Consulting and Clinical Psychology, 72,* 870–878.

McCrady, B. S., Epstein, E. E., & Hirsch, L. S. (1999). Maintaining change after conjoint behavioral alcohol treatment for men: Outcomes at six months. *Addiction, 94,* 1381–1396.

McCrady, B. S., Moreau, J., Paolino, T. J., & Longabaugh, R. (1982). Joint hospitalization and couples' therapy for alcoholism: Four-year outcomes. *Journal of Studies on Alcohol, 43,* 1244–1250.

McCrady, B. S., Noel, N. E., Stout, R. L., Abrams, D. B., Fisher-Nelson, H., & Hay, W. (1986). Comparative effectiveness of three types of spouse involvement in outpatient behavioral alcoholism treatment. *Journal of Studies on Alcohol, 47,* 459–467.

McCrady, B. S., Noel, N. E., Stout, R. L., Abrams, D. B., & Nelson, H. F. (1991). Effectiveness of three types of spouse-involved behavioral alcoholism treatment: Outcome 18 months after treatment. *British Journal of Addictions, 86,* 1415–1424.

McCrady, B. S., Paolino, T. J., Longabaugh, R. L., & Rossi, J. (1979). Effects of joint hospital admission and couples treatment for hospitalized alcoholics: A pilot study. *Addictive Behaviors, 4,* 155–165.

Miller, W. R. (1996). *Form 90. A structured assessment interview for drinking and related behaviors.* In M. E. Mattson, & L. A. Marshall (Eds.),

Project MATCH monograph series (Vol. 5). Bethesda, MD: National Institute on Alcohol Abuse and Alcoholism, U.S. Department of Health and Human Services.

Miller, W. R. (2004). *Combined behavioral intervention manual: A clinical research guide for therapists treating people with alcohol abuse and dependence.* NIH Pub. No. 04-5288. Rockville, MD: National Institute on Alcohol Abuse and Alcoholism.

Miller, W. R., & Marlatt, G. A. (1984). *Comprehensive Drinker Profile.* Odessa, FL: Psychological Assessment Resources.

Miller, W. R., & Rollnick, S. (2002). *Motivational interviewing* (2nd ed.). New York, NY: Guilford Press.

Miller, W. R., Sovereign, R. G., & Krege, B. (1988). Motivational interviewing with problem drinkers: 2. The Drinker's Check-up as a preventive intervention. *Behavioural Psychotherapy, 16,* 251–268.

Miller, W. R., Tonigan, J. S., & Longabaugh, R. (1995). The Drinker Inventory of Consequences (DrInC): An instrument for assessing adverse consequences of alcohol abuse (Vol 4., Project Match Monograph Series). NIH Publication No. 95-3911. Rockville, MD: US Department of Health and Human Services, Public Health Service, Notional Institutes of Health, National Institute on Alcohol Abuse and Alcoholism,.

Miller, W. R., Walters, S. T., & Bennett, M. E. (2001). How effective is alcoholism treatment in the United States? *Journal of Studies on Alcohol, 62,* 211–220.

Miller, W. R., & Wilbourne, P. L. (2002). Mesa Grande: A methodological analysis of clinical trials of treatment for alcohol use disorders. *Addiction, 97,* 265–277.

Miller, W. R., Zweben, A., DiClemente, C. C., & Rychtarik, R. G. (1994). *Motivational enhancement therapy manual.* NIH Pub. No. 94-3723. Rockville, MD: National Institute on Alcohol Abuse and Alcoholism.

Moos, R. H., & Billings, A. (1982). Children of alcoholics during the recovery process: Alcoholic and matched control families. *Addictive Behaviors, 7,* 155–163.

Moos, R. H., Finney, J. W., & Gamble, W. (1982). The process of recovery from alcoholism: II. Comparing spouses of alcoholic patients and matched community controls. *Journal of Studies on Alcohol, 43,* 888–909.

Morgan, T. J., Epstein, E. E., McCrady, B. S., Cook, S. M., Jensen, N. K., & Kelly, S. (unpublished paper). Treatment engagement and retention in outpatient alcoholism treatment for women.

O'Farrell, T. J. (1993). A behavioral marital therapy couples group program for alcoholics and their spouses. In T. J. O'Farrell (Ed.), *Treating alcohol problems: Marital and family interventions* (pp. 127–209). New York, NY: Guilford Press.

O'Farrell, T. J., Choquette, K. A., & Cutter, H. S. G. (1998). Couples relapse prevention sessions after behavioral marital therapy for male alcoholics: Outcomes during the three years after starting treatment. *Journal of Studies on Alcohol, 59*, 357–370.

O'Farrell, T. J., Choquette, K. A., Cutter, H. S. G., Floyd, F. J., Bayog, R., Brown, E. D., et al. (1996). Cost-benefit and cost-effectiveness analyses of behavioral marital therapy as an addition to outpatient alcoholism treatment. *Journal of Substance Abuse, 8*, 145–166.

O'Farrell, T. J., Murphy, C. M., Stephan, S. H., Fals-Stewart, W., & Murphy, M. (2004). Partner violence before and after couples-based alcoholism treatment for male alcoholic patients: The role of treatment involvement and abstinence. *Journal of Consulting and Clinical Psychology, 72*, 202–217.

O'Malley, S. S., Jaffe, A. J., Change, G., Schottenfeld, R. S., Meyer, R. E., & Rounsaville, B. (1992). Naltrexone and coping skills therapy for alcohol dependence: A controlled study. *Archives of General Psychiatry, 49*, 881–887.

Paille, F. M., Guelfi, J. D., Perkins, A. C., Royer, R. J., Steru, L., & Parot, P. (1995). Double-blind randomized multicentre trial of acamprosate in maintaining abstinence from alcohol. *Alcohol & Alcoholism, 30*(2), 239–247.

Project MATCH Research Group. (1997a). Matching alcoholism treatments to client heterogeneity: Project MATCH posttreatment drinking outcomes. *Journal of Studies on Alcohol, 58*, 7–29.

Project MATCH Research Group. (1997b). Project MATCH secondary a priori hypotheses. *Addiction, 92*, 1671–1698.

Rosenthal, R. N., & Westreich, L. (1999). Treatment of persons with dual diagnoses of substance use disorder and other psychological problems. In B. S. McCrady, & E. E. Epstein (Eds.), *Addictions: A comprehensive guidebook* (pp. 439–476). New York, NY: Oxford University Press.

Sobell, L. C., & Sobell, M. B. (1996). *Timeline Followback: A calendar method for assessing alcohol and drug use (Users Guide)*. Toronto: Addiction Research Foundation.

Sobell, L. C., Agrawal, S., Sobell, M. B., Leo, G. I., Young, L. J., Cunningham, J. A., et al. (2003). Comparison of a quick drinking screen with the Timeline Followback for individuals with alcohol problems. *Journal of Studies on Alcohol, 64*, 858–861.

Spanier, G. B. (1976). Measuring dyadic adjustment: New scales for assessing the quality of marriage and similar dyads. *Journal of Marriage and the Family, 38*, 15–28.

Steinglass, P., Weiner, S., & Mendelson, J. H. (1971). A systems approach to alcoholism: A model and its clinical application. *Archives of General Psychiatry, 24*, 401–408.

U.S. Department of Health and Human Services (2001). *10th special report to the U. S. Congress on alcohol and health from the Secretary of Health and Human Services* (2000). Washington, DC: U.S. Department of Health and Human Services, National Institute on Alcohol Abuse and Alcoholism.

U.S. Department of Health and Human Services, National Institutes of Health. (2003). *Alcohol: A women's health issue.* NIH Publication number 03-4956. Washington, DC: U.S. Department of Health and Human Services, National Institute on Alcohol Abuse and Alcoholism.

Volpicelli, J. R., Alterman, A. I., Hayashida, M., & O'Brien, C. P. (1992). Naltrexone in the treatment of alcohol dependence. *Archives of General Psychiatry, 49*, 876–880.

Yi, H.-Y., Chen, C. M., & Williams, G. D. (2006). *Surveillance Report #76: Trends in alcohol-related fatal traffic crashes, United States, 1982–2004.* Bethesda, MD: US Department of Health and Human Services.

Zitter, R., & McCrady, B. S. (1979). *The Drinking Patterns Questionnaire.* Unpublished manuscript.

Zweig, R. S., McCrady, B. S., & Epstein, E. E. (2008). Investigation of the psychometric properties of the Drinking Patterns Questionnaire. *Addictive Disorders and Their Treatment, 7*.

About the Authors

Barbara S. McCrady received her BS in Biological Sciences from Purdue University in 1969 and her PhD in Psychology from the University of Rhode Island in 1975. She is currently Distinguished Professor of Psychology and Director of the Center on Alcoholism, Substance Abuse, and Addictions at the University of New Mexico. Previously, she was the chair of the Department of Psychology and Clinical Director of the Center of Alcohol Studies at Rutgers University.

Dr. McCrady is an internationally known expert in empirically supported treatments for persons with substance-use disorders, with a particular focus on conjoint therapy, cognitive-behavioral therapy (CBT), mutual help groups, and therapies for women. She is a fellow of the Clinical Psychology and Addictions divisions of the American Psychological Association (APA). She is a past president of Division 50 (Addictions) of the APA, past member of the Board of Directors of the Research Society on Alcoholism, and past secretary-treasurer of the Association for Behavioral and Cognitive Therapies. She also served on the Research Advisory Board of the Hazelden Foundation and the Board of Directors of the Pacific Institute for Research and Evaluation. She has served on a National Institute on Alcohol Abuse and Alcoholism (NIAAA) study section and has also served on advisory panels for NIAAA, the National Institute on Drug Abuse, and the Institute of Medicine. Her work has been funded by the National Institutes of Health (NIH) since 1979, and was funded under the NIAAA MERIT program for 10 years. Dr. McCrady has published close to 200 refereed papers, chapters, and books on her work.

Dr. McCrady is the 1999 recipient of the AMERSA Betty Ford award and the 2007 recipient of the outstanding educator award from Division 50 of the APA.

Elizabeth E. Epstein received her PhD in Clinical Psychology from the University of Connecticut in 1989. She is a licensed psychologist, and an Associate Research Professor in the Clinical Division at the Center of Alcohol Studies, Rutgers University. She holds joint appointments with the Graduate School of Applied and Professional Psychology (GSAPP), the Graduate Faculty in the Department of Psychology at Rutgers, and the University of Medicine and Dentistry of New Jersey/Robert Wood Johnson Medical School Department of Psychiatry Addictions Psychiatry Division. In addition to her academic and research activities, Dr. Epstein treats patients part time. Dr. Epstein also directs the Program for Addictions, Consultation, and Treatment (PACT), jointly run by the Rutgers Center of Alcohol Studies and GSAPP. PACT is an outpatient clinic for treatment of substance abuse, providing individual, group, couples, or family therapy for substance abusers and their family members. Dr. Epstein is an expert in cognitive-behavioral (CBT) individual- and couples-therapy development for alcohol and drug abuse and dependence. She has lectured widely, presenting research findings at both scientific conferences and training workshops in CBT for addictions. Dr. Epstein is a member of the Research Society on Alcoholism, Association for Behavioral and Cognitive Therapies, and the APA. She serves as ad hoc grant reviewer for NIAAA and NIDA, and reviews manuscripts for many scientific journals. She is also a member of the editorial board of the *Journal of Studies on Alcohol and Drugs*. Dr. Epstein is recipient of NIAAA- and NIDA-funded grants to develop and test couples, group, and individual CBT models and mechanisms of treatment for alcohol- and drug-dependent men and women, as well as to study individual differences among substance abusers in comorbidity, family history, and other potential indicators of heterogeneity in clinical presentation and response to treatment for addictions. Dr. Epstein has been published extensively in scientific journals on the addictions.